A CATECHISM OF MODERNISM

A CATECHISM OF MODERNISM

by

The Rev. J. B. Lemius, O.M.I.

FOUNDED ON THE ENCYCLICAL

PASCENDI DOMINICI GREGIS
(On Modernism)
By Pope Pius X

"We must now break silence, in order to expose before the whole Church, in their true colors, those men who have assumed this bad disguise."

Translated from the French at St. Joseph's Seminary, Dunwoodie, New York.

TAN BOOKS AND PUBLISHERS, INC.
Rockford, Illinois

1981

Nihil Obstat

REV. REMY LAFORT

Censor Librorum

Imprimatur

✠ JOHN M. FARLEY

Archbishop of New York

March 19, 1908

Originally published by the Society For The Propagation of the Faith, Archdiocese of New York.

Reprinted by TAN Books and Publishers, Inc., Rockford, Illinois, with permission from the Propagation of the Faith, Archdiocese of New York.

ISBN: 0-89555-167-5

Library of Congress Catalog Card No. 81-52536

Printed in the United States of America

TAN BOOKS AND PUBLISHERS, INC.
P.O. Box 424
Rockford, Illinois 61105

1981

LETTER OF
HIS EMINENCE CARDINAL MERRY DEL VAL
TO THE AUTHOR

Your Reverence:

A high commendation, and, at the same time, an expression of keenest satisfaction is what I have the pleasure of forwarding to your Reverence, in the name of the Sovereign Pontiff, after handing him the splendid brochure bearing the title, "*Catechism of Modernism, founded upon the Encyclical,* Pascendi Dominici Gregis."

The character of the pontifical document, and the nature of the errors therein condemned, might perhaps render difficult a complete and ready understanding of the important Encyclical in its every detail. I speak for the less cultured classes, and for those who are strangers to the movement of good, as well as of evil, doctrines. Unhappily they fall a very easy prey to all errors, especially when these errors are presented under a false scientific guise. Nor are they, on the other hand, sufficiently wide awake to understand, as readily, the cause of the evil.

Hence you have accomplished a remarkably useful work, by resolving the document into questions, according to the simple and plain method of your Catechism. Thereby you bring it within the intellectual grasp of the less cultured.

His Holiness views with complacency the spirited and fruitful work of your Reverence, and he commends you for still another reason—to wit, that you have in no wise departed from the letter of the Encyclical. He hopes to see the product of your timely study obtain a wide circulation, and accords you from his heart the Apostolic Benediction.

Communicating these sentiments to you, I thank you for the copy of the brochure which you have so kindly sent me. With assurance of sincerest esteem, I am your Reverence's

Very devoted servant,

R. CARD. MERRY DEL VAL.

ROME, *December* 14, 1907.

TRANSLATOR'S NOTE

The present translation of the *Catéchisme du Modernisme* of Father Lemius has been prepared with the intention of helping to carry out the desire of the Holy Father that the Encyclical *Pascendi Dominici Gregis* be made as well known as possible to the entire flock, and to meet, in that respect, what seems to be a real need on the part of our Catholic laymen. The questions dealt with in the Encyclical refer to deep and arduous problems of theology and philosophy, a circumstance which makes the full import of the document difficult to be grasped save by the trained mind of the theologian; whence it is not surprising that the question is repeatedly asked: "What is this Modernism of which we are hearing so much?" This ignorance of the subject on the part of our American Catholic laymen is, at least, gratifying evidence, if such were needed, that Modernism has not in fact penetrated into the ranks of our people, but it is a wise precaution, and in strict accordance with the intentions of our Holy Father, the Pope, to have the faithful put upon their guard against this "synthesis of all the heresies," and to inform them as to its real nature, so that they may be able to detect its subtle presence in the various forms of literature that have been influenced by its spirit.

The catechetical method has long been recognized as the most appropriate and effectual when it is question of imparting popular instruction, and it is hoped that the present little treatise may prove a useful supplement to the systematic oral instructions on Modernism which are being given in our churches and academic institutions. The answers to practically all the questions have been taken verbatim from the text of the Encyclical, and thus the learner will have the filial satisfaction of knowing that he is being instructed in the very words of the Holy Father himself. In this manner the Encyclical will doubtless be read and studied by many who might not feel themselves equal to the task of mastering it in its original form.

The text used in preparing the translation is taken from the September-December number of *The New York Review*, being a reproduction of the one previously published in the *London Tablet*.

St. Joseph's Seminary, Dunwoodie, N. Y.
Feast of St. Gabriel, 1908.

CONTENTS

PART I

THE MODERNIST ERRORS.

CHAPTER I.

CONTENTS

CHAPTER II.

CHAPTER III.

CHAPTER IV.

THE RELIGIOUS PHILOSOPHY OF THE MODERNISTS (CONTINUED).

CONTENTS

Chapter V.

Chapter VI.

Chapter VII.

Chapter VIII.

CONTENTS

PART II

THE CAUSE OF MODERNISM

PART III

REMEDIES.

CONCLUSION

A CATECHISM OF MODERNISM

PREAMBLE

GRAVITY OF THE MODERNIST ERRORS

Q. What is the first duty assigned to the Sovereign Pontiff by Our Lord Jesus Christ?

A. His Holiness, Pius X, answers for us: The office divinely committed to Us of feeding the Lord's flock, has especially this duty assigned to it by Christ, namely, to guard with the greatest vigilance the deposit of the faith delivered to the saints, rejecting the profane novelties of words and oppositions of knowledge falsely so called.

Q. Was not this vigilance necessary in every age?

A. There has never been a time when this watchfulness of the supreme pastor was not necessary to the Catholic body; for, owing to the efforts of the enemy of the human race, there have never been lacking " men speaking perverse things " (Acts xx. 30), " vain talkers and seducers " (Tit. i. 10), " erring and driving into error " (2 Tim. iii. 13).

Q. Are these misguided men more numerous to-day? What is their aim?

A. It must be confessed that the number of the enemies of the cross of Christ has in these last days increased exceedingly, men who are striving, by arts entirely new and full of subtlety, to destroy the vital energy of the Church, and, if they can, to ov   ·ow utterly Christ's kingdom itself.

Q. Why may the Sovereign Pontiff remain silent no longer?

A. We may no longer be silent, he says, lest We should seem to fail in Our most sacred duty, and lest the kindness that, in the hope of wiser counsels, We have hitherto shown them, should be attributed to forgetfulness of Our office.

Q. Where are the "partisans of error" to be found? Are they open enemies?

A. That We make no delay in this matter is rendered necessary especially by the fact that the partisans of error are to be sought not only among the Church's open enemies; they lie hid, a thing to be deeply deplored and feared, in her very bosom and heart, and are the more mischievous the less conspicuously they appear.

Q. Holy Father, are these hidden enemies, who cause anxiety to your paternal heart, to be found among Catholics? Are they found in the ranks of the priesthood?

A. Yes. Many belong to the Catholic laity; nay, and this is far more lamentable, many belong to the ranks of the priesthood itself, who, feigning a love for the Church, lacking the firm protection of philosophy and theology, nay more, thoroughly imbued with the poisonous doctrines taught by the enemies of the Church, and lost to all sense of modesty, *vaunt themselves as reformers* of the Church.

Q. Do these lay Catholics and priests, who pose as reformers of the Church, dare to attack Christ's work? Do they even attack the very Person of Our Lord and Saviour, Jesus Christ?

A. Forming more boldly into line of attack, they assail all that is most sacred in the work of Christ, not sparing even the Person of the Divine Redeemer, whom, with sacrilegious daring, they reduce to a simple, mere man.

Q. Are those men surprised when Your Holiness numbers them among the enemies of Holy Church?

A. Though they express astonishment themselves, no one can justly be surprised that We number such men among the enemies of the Church, if, leaving out of consideration the internal disposition of soul, of which God alone is the judge, he is acquainted with their tenets, their manner of speech, their conduct. Nor indeed will he err in accounting them the most pernicious of all the adversaries of the Church.

Q. Why, Holy Father, do you call them the bitterest enemies of the Church?

A. For this reason: As We have said, they put their designs for her ruin into operation not from without but from within; hence, the danger is present almost in the very veins and heart of the Church, whose injury is the more certain, the more intimate is their knowledge of her.

Q. Are there still further grounds for calling these men the Church's bitterest enemies?

A. Yes. They lay the axe not to the branches and shoots, but to the very root, that is, to the faith and its deepest fibers.

Q. Do they "withhold their hands when they have struck at the root" of life?

A. Having struck at this root of immortality, they proceed to disseminate poison through the whole tree, so that there is no part of Catholic truth from which they hold their hand, none that they do not strive to corrupt.

Q. How do they pursue their purpose? What tactics do they employ?

A. None is more skilful, none more astute than they, in the employment of a thousand noxious arts; for they double the parts of rationalist and Catholic, and this so craftily that they easily lead the unwary into error.

Q. Should not Catholic laymen and priests fear and recoil from the consequences of these doctrines?

A. The consequences should make them hesitate; but, since audacity is their characteristic, there is no conclusion of any kind from which they shrink or which they do not thrust forward with pertinacity and assurance.

Q. Why are they particularly dangerous and calculated to " deceive souls?"

A. They are indeed well calculated to deceive souls, because they lead a life of the greatest activity, of assiduous and ardent application to every branch of learning, and because they possess, as a rule, a reputation for the strictest morality.

Q. Holy Father, do you hope to cure these misguided ones?

A. This almost destroys all hope of cure: their very doctrines have given such a bent to their minds, that they disdain all authority and brook no restraint; and relying upon a false conscience, they attempt to ascribe to a love of truth that which is in reality the result of pride and obstinacy.

Q. Holy Father, have you no hope of recalling these misguided individuals to a better sense?

A. Once indeed We had hopes of recalling them to a better sense, and to this end We first of all showed them kindness as Our children, then We treated them with severity, and at last We have had recourse, though with great reluctance, to public reproof. But you know how fruitless has been Our action. They bowed their head for a moment, but it was soon uplifted more arrogantly than ever.

Q. Since all hope of reclaiming these enemies is lost, why, Holy Father, do you raise your voice in warning?

A. If it were a matter which concerned them alone, We might perhaps have overlooked it: but the security of the Catholic name is at stake. Wherefore, to maintain it longer, would be a crime.

Q. *It is now time to speak?*

A. We must now break silence, in order to expose before the whole Church in their true colors those men who have assumed this bad disguise.

Q. *By what name may we call these new enemies of Jesus Christ and of His Holy Church?*

A. They are commonly and rightly called "Modernists."

END AND DIVISION OF THE ENCYCLICAL.

Q. *Give the end and division of the Encyclical?*

A. Since the Modernists employ a very clever artifice, namely, to present their doctrines without order and systematic arrangement into one whole, scattered and disjointed one from another, so as to appear to be in doubt and uncertainty, while they are in reality firm and steadfast, it will be of advantage to bring their teachings together here into one group, and to point out the connection between them, and thus to pass to an examination of the sources of the errors, and to prescribe remedies for averting the evil.

PART I
The Modernist Errors

PART II
The Causes of the Modernist Errors

PART III
Remedies for the Modernist Errors

PART I

THE MODERNIST ERRORS

PRELUDE.

Q. To proceed in an orderly manner in the exposition of the errors of Modernism, how many personalities must we consider in the Modernist?

A. To proceed in an orderly manner in this recondite subject, it must first of all be noted that every Modernist sustains and comprises within himself many personalities; he is a philosopher, a believer, a theologian, an historian, a critic, an apologist, a reformer. These rôles must be clearly distinguished from one another by all who would accurately know their system and thoroughly comprehend the principles and the consequences of their doctrines.

CHAPTER I.

The Religious Philosophy of the Modernists.

§1. *Agnosticism.*

Q. We begin, then, with the philosopher. What doctrine do the Modernists use as the foundation for their religious philosophy?

A. Modernists place the foundation of religious

philosophy in that doctrine which is usually called *Agnosticism.*

Q. Give the teaching of Agnosticism?

A. According to this teaching, human reason is confined entirely within the field of *phenomena,* that is to say, to things that are perceptible to the senses, and in the manner in which they are perceptible: it has no right and no power to transgress these limits. Hence it is incapable of lifting itself up to God, and of recognizing His existence, even by means of visible things.

Q. What conclusions do Modernists draw from this doctrine?

A. From this it is inferred that God can never be the direct object of science, and that, as regards history, He must not be considered as an historical subject.

Q. What, according to these premises, will become of natural theology, the motives of credibility, and of external revelation?

A. Given these premises, all will readily perceive what becomes of *natural theology,* of the *motives of credibility,* of *external revelation.* The Modernists simply make away with them altogether; they include them in *Intellectualism,* which they call a ridiculous and long ago defunct system.

Q. Do the condemnations of the Church exercise any restraint on the Modernists?

A. Nor does the fact that the Church has formally condemned these portentous errors exercise the slightest restraint upon them.

Q. What definition of the Vatican Council may be cited against the Modernists?

A. The Vatican Council has defined: If any one says that the one true God, Our Creator and Lord, can not be known with certainty by the natural light of human reason by means of the things that are made, let him be anathema (*De Revel.,* can. 1); and also: If any one says that it is not possible or not expedient that man be taught, through the medium of divine revelation, about God and the worship to be paid Him, let him be anathema (*Ibid.,* can. 2); and finally: If any one says that divine revelation can not be made credible by external signs, and that therefore men should be drawn to the faith only by their personal internal experience or by private inspiration, let him be anathema (*De Fide,* can. 3).

Q. But how can the Modernists make the transition from Agnosticism, which is a state of pure nescience, to scientific and historic Atheism, which is a doctrine of positive denial; and consequently, by what legitimate process of reasoning, starting from ignorance as to whether God has in fact intervened in the history of the human race or not, do they proceed, in their explanation of this history, to ignore God altogether, as if He really had not intervened?

23

A. The matter may be understood from this: It is a fixed and established principle among them that both science and history must be atheistic: and within their boundaries there is room for nothing but *phenomena;* God and all that is divine are utterly excluded.

Q. According to this absurd teaching, what must be held regarding the sacred Person of Christ, what concerning the mysteries of His life and death, of His Resurrection and Ascension into heaven?

A. All this we shall soon see.

§2. *Vital Immanence.*

Q. From what you have just said, it is clear that "Agnosticism is but the negative part of the system of the Modernists." Will you give the positive side?

A. The positive side of it consists in what they call *vital immanence.*

Q. How do the Modernists advance from Agnosticism to immanence?

A. This is how they advance from one to the other: Religion, whether natural or supernatural, must, like every other fact, admit of some explanation. But when natural theology has been destroyed, the road to revelation closed through the rejection of the arguments of credibility, and all external revelation absolutely denied, it is clear that this explanation will be sought in vain outside man himself. It must, therefore, be looked for *in* man; and since religion is a form of life, the explanation must certainly be found in the life of man. Hence the principle of *religious immanence* is formulated.

Q. It seems that the Modernist partisans of Agnosticism can find only in man and in his life the explanation of religion. Now, to explain this vital immanence, what do they give as the first stimulus and the first manifestation of all vital phenomena, but particularly of religion?

A. The first actuation, so to say, of every vital phenomenon—and religion, as has been said, belongs to this category—is due to a certain necessity or impulsion; but it has its origin, speaking more particularly of life, in a movement of the heart, which movement is called a *sentiment.*

Q. Whence, according to this, originates the principle of faith and, consequently, the principle of religion?

A. Since God is the object of religion, we must conclude that faith, which is the basis and the foundation of all religion, consists in a sentiment which originates from a need of the divine.

Q. Does this "need of the divine," according to Modernists, appertain to the domain of consciousness?

A. This need of the divine, which is experienced only in special and favorable circumstances, can not, of itself, appertain to the domain of consciousness.

Q.   Where is this " need of the divine" latent?

A.   It is at first latent within the consciousness, or, to borrow a term from modern philosophy, in the *subconsciousness,* where also its roots lie hidden and undetected.

§3.   Origin of Religion in General.

Q.   Should any one ask how it is that this need of the divine which man experiences within himself grows up into a religion, what do the Modernists reply?

A.   The Modernists reply thus: Science and history, they say, are confined within two limits, the one external, namely, the visible world, the other internal, which is consciousness. When one or other of these boundaries has been reached, there can be no further progress, for beyond is the *unknowable.* In presence of this *unknowable,* whether it is outside man and beyond the visible world of nature, or lies hidden within in the *subconsciousness,* the need of the divine, according to the principles of *Fideism,* excites in a soul with a propensity toward religion a certain special *sentiment,* without any previous advertence of the mind: and this sentiment possesses, implied within itself both as its own object and as its intrinsic cause, the *reality* of the divine, and in a way unites man with God. It is this sentiment to which Modernists give the name of faith, and this it is which they consider the beginning of religion.

§4. *Notion of Revelation.*

*Q. Is Modernist philosophy confined to the above
mentioned system?*

A. We have not yet come to the end of their
philosophy, or, to speak more accurately, their folly.

*Q. What do the Modernists find in their pretended
" sentiment of the divine?"*

A. Modernism finds in this *sentiment* not faith
only, but with and in faith, as they understand it,
revelation, they say, abides.

Q. Do they find revelation?

A. What more, they say, can one require for revelation? Is not that religious *sentiment* which is perceptible in the consciousness, revelation, or at least the
beginning of revelation? Nay, is not God Himself,
as He manifests Himself to the soul, indistinctly it is
true, in this same religious sense, revelation? And
they add: Since God is both the object and the cause
of faith, this revelation is at the same time *of* God and
from God; that is, God is both the revealer and the revealed.

*Q. What absurd doctrine flows from this philos-
ophy, or rather, from this Modernist raving?*

A. Hence springs that ridiculous proposition of the
Modernists, that every religion, according to the different aspect under which it is viewed, must be considered as both natural and supernatural.

Q. What follows from this?

A. Hence it is that they make consciousness and revelation synonymous.

Q. What supreme and universal law would the Modernists derive from this doctrine?

A. The law according to which *religious consciousness* is given as the universal rule, to be put on an equal footing with revelation, and to which all must submit.

Q. Must everything, even the supreme authority of the Church, be subjected to this law?

A. Yes, all things must be made subject, even the supreme authority of the Church, whether in its teaching capacity, or in that of legislator in the province of sacred liturgy or discipline.

§5. *Transformation and· Deformation of Phenomena by Faith.*

Q. What more is requisite in order to give a complete idea of the origin of the faith and of revelation, as the Modernists understand the matter?

A. In all this process, from which, according to the Modernists, faith and revelation spring, *one point is to be particularly noted*, for it is of capital importance on account of the historico-critical corollaries which are deduced from it.

Q. How does the "unknowable" of the Modernist philosophy, as above explained, present itself to faith?

A. The unknowable they talk of does not present itself to faith as something solitary and isolated; but rather in close conjunction with some phenomenon, which, though it belongs to the realm of science and history, yet to some extent oversteps their bounds.

Q. What is this phenomenon?

A. Such a phenomenon may be a fact of nature containing within itself something mysterious; or it may be a man, whose character, actions and words can not, apparently, be reconciled with the ordinary laws of history.

Q. In this union of the " unknowable " with phenomenon, what is the result for faith?

A. Faith, attracted by the unknowable, which is united with the phenomenon, possesses itself of the whole phenomenon, and, as it were, permeates it with its own life.

Q. From this possession of phenomenon by faith, and from the permeation of life, what follows?

A. From this two things follow.

Q. What is the first?

A. The first is a sort of *transfiguration* of the phenomenon, by its elevation above its own true conditions, by which it becomes more adapted to that form of the divine which faith will infuse into it.

Q. What is the second?

A. The second is a kind of *disfigurement,* which springs from the fact that faith, which has made the phenomenon independent of the circumstances of place and time, attributes to it qualities which it has not.

Q. Upon what phenomena, according to the Modernists, does this double work of transformation and deformation particularly act?

A. This is true particularly of the phenomena of the past, and the older they are, the truer it is.

Q. What laws do the Modernists deduce for this twofold operation?

A. From these two principles the Modernists deduce two laws, which, when united with a third which they have already got from Agnosticism, constitute the foundation of historical criticism.

Q. Give an example of these three laws?

A. We will take an illustration from the Person of Christ. In the Person of Christ, they say, science and history encounter nothing that is not human. Therefore, in virtue of the first canon deduced from Agnosticism, whatever there is in His history suggestive of the divine, must be rejected. Then, according to the second canon, the historical Person of Christ was transfigured by faith; therefore everything that raises it above historical conditions must be removed. Lastly, the third canon, which lays down that the Person of Christ has been *disfigured* by faith, requires that everything should be excluded, deeds and words and all else that is not in keeping with His character, circumstances, and education, and with the place and time in which He lived.

Q. Is not this a strange style of reasoning?

A. A strange style of reasoning, truly; but it is
<u>Modernist criticism</u>.

§6. *Origin of Religions in Particular.*

Q. Is "religious sentiment" then, to use a Modernist expression, the true germ and complete explanation of all that is in religion?

A. The *religious sentiment,* which through the agency of *vital immanence* emerges from the lurking-places of the subconsciousness, is the *germ* of all religion, and the *explanation* of everything that has been or ever will be in any religion.

Q. How does this "religious sentiment" mature?

A. This *sentiment,* which was at first only rudimentary and almost formless, gradually matured under the influence of that mysterious principle from which it originated, with the progress of human life, of which, as has been said, it is a form.

Q. Do all religions, according to the Modernists, originate in this manner?

A. This is the origin of all religion.

Q. Must we say the same even of supernatural religions?

A. Yes—even of supernatural religion: it is only a development of this *religious sentiment.*

Q. But do not the Modernists make an exception for the Catholic religion?

A. No; the Catholic religion is not an exception; it is quite on a level with the rest.

Q. By what process and in whose " consciousness " do they say that the Catholic religion was engendered?

A. It was engendered by the process of *vital immanence,* in the *consciousness* of Christ, who was a man of the choicest nature, whose like has never been, nor will be.

Q. Is not this blasphemy?

A. Those who hear these audacious, these sacrilegious assertions, are simply shocked!

Q. Surely, Holy Father, none but scoffers can hold such doctrines. Is it possible that priests follow this " foolish babbling? "

A. Ah, replies the Sovereign Pontiff, these are not merely the foolish babblings of infidels. There are *many Catholics, yea, and priests, too,* who say these things openly; and they boast that they are going to reform the Church by these ravings!

Q. Does not Modernism seem to be " the old error " of Pelagius?

A. There is no question now of *the old error,* by which a sort of right to the supernatural order was claimed for the human nature. We have gone far beyond that.

Q. Explain?

A. We have reached the point when it is affirmed that our most holy religion, *in the man Christ as in us,*

32

emanated from nature spontaneously and entirely. Than this there is surely nothing more destructive of the whole supernatural order.

Q. Quote the Vatican Council on this doctrine?

A. The Vatican Council most justly decreed: If any one says that man can not be raised by God to a knowledge and perfection which surpasses nature, but that he can and should, by his own efforts and by a constant development, attain finally to the possession of all truth and good, let him be anathema (*De Revel.*, can. 3).

§7. *Action of the Intellect in Faith.*

Q. Do the Modernists find faith only in sentiment? Has not the intellect its part in the act of faith?

A. So far there has been no mention of the intellect. Still it also, according to the teaching of the Modernists, has its part in *the act of faith.* And it is of importance to see how.

Q. Does " sentiment," according to the Modernists, suffice to give us God, the object and author of faith?

A. In that *sentiment* of which We have frequently spoken, since sentiment is not knowledge, God indeed presents Himself to man, but in a manner so confused and indistinct that He can hardly be perceived by the believer.

Q. What is further required by " sentiment?"

A. It is necessary that a ray of light should be cast upon this sentiment, so that God may be clearly distinguished and set apart from it.

Q. Is this "enlightenment," then, the task of the intellect in the Modernist act of faith?

A. This is the task of the intellect, whose office it is to reflect and to analyze, and by means of which man first transforms into mental pictures the vital phenomena which arise within him, and then expresses them in words. Hence the common saying of Modernists: that the religious man must *ponder* his faith.

Q. Give the comparisons employed by the Modernist to explain the action of the "intellect" when it encounters "sentiment" in the act of faith?

A. The intellect, encountering this sentiment, directs itself upon it, and produces in it a work resembling that of a painter who restores and gives new life to a picture that has perished with age. The simile is that of one of the leaders of Modernism.

Q. What is the "operation" of the intellect in the production of the act of faith?

A. The operation of the intellect in this work is a double one.

Q. Give the first operation?

A. The intellect first, by a natural and spontaneous act, expresses its concepts in a simple, ordinary statement.

Q. And the second?

A. Then, on reflection and deeper consideration, or, as they say, *by elaborating its thought,* the intellect expresses the idea in *secondary* propositions, which are derived from the first, but are more perfect and distinct.

Q. How can these formulas, the fruit of intellect's labor on its own thought, become " dogmas?"

A. These *secondary* propositions, if they finally receive the approval of the supreme magisterium of the Church, *constitute dogma.*

§8. *Dogma.*

Q. Is not dogma the principal point of the Modernists' system?

A. We have reached one of the principal points in the Modernists' system, namely, the origin and the nature of dogma.

Q. What, then, for the Modernists, is " origin of dogma?"

A. They place the *origin of dogma* in those primitive and simple formulæ which, under a certain aspect, are necessary to faith; for revelation, to be truly such, requires the clear manifestation of God in the consciousness. But dogma itself, they apparently hold, is contained in the *secondary* formulæ.

Q. According to Modernist notions, how shall we ascertain the nature of dogma?

A. To *ascertain the nature of dogma,* we must first

find the relation which exists between the *religious formulas* and the *religious sentiment.*

Q. How shall we find this relation?

A. This will be readily perceived by him who realizes that these *formulas* have no other purpose than to furnish the believer with a means of giving an account of his faith to himself.

Q. Do the formulas " stand between the believer and his faith?"

A. These formulas, therefore, stand midway between the believer and his faith; in their relation to the faith, they are the inadequate expression of its object, and are usually called *symbols;* in their relation to the believer, they are mere *instruments.*

Q. What shall we say of the truth expressed in these formulas?

A. It is quite impossible to maintain that they express absolute truth.

Q. In so far as they are symbols, what are these formulas for the Modernist?

A. In so far as they are *symbols,* they are the images of truth, and so must be adapted to the religious sentiment in its relation to man.

Q. As " instruments," what are " symbols?"

A. As *instruments,* they are the vehicles of truth, and must therefore in their turn be adapted to man in his relation to the religious sentiment.

§9. *Variability of Dogma.*

Q. Are these dogmatic formulas—symbols of the faith and instruments of belief—invariable?

A. The object of the *religious sentiment,* since it embraces the *absolute,* possesses an *infinite variety of aspects,* of which now one, now another, may present itself. In like manner, he who believes may pass through different phases. Consequently, the formulæ too, which we call dogmas, must be subject to these vicissitudes, and are, therefore, liable to change.

Q. Is there an intrinsic evolution of dogma?

A. Thus the way is open to the *intrinsic evolution* of dogma. An immense collection of sophisms this, that ruins and destroys all religion.

Q. Is not this intrinsic evolution of dogma possible, nay, rather, necessary?

A. Dogma is not only able, but *ought to evolve and to be changed.* This is strongly affirmed by the Modernists, and as clearly flows from their principles.

Q. From what fundamental principle do the Modernists deduce the necessity of intrinsic evolution in dogmas?

A. Among the chief points of their teaching is this which they deduce from the principle of *vital immanence;* that religious formulas, to be really religious and not merely theological speculations, ought to be living and to live the life of the religious sentiment.

Q. Since these formulas must be animated by the very life of religious sentiment, should they not be made for religious sentiment?

A. This is not to be understood in the sense that these formulas, especially if merely imaginative, were to be made for the religious sentiment; it has no more to do with their origin than with number or quality; what is necessary is that the religious sentiment, which, when needful, introduced some modifications, should vitally assimilate them.

Q. What is " vital assimilation" by sentiment?

A. In other words, it is necessary that the primitive formula be accepted and *sanctioned by the heart;* and similarly the subsequent work from which spring the secondary formulas must proceed under the guidance of the heart.

Q. How does the necessity of vital assimilation induce substantial variation of dogma?

A. These formulas, to be living, should be, and should remain, adapted to the faith and to him who believes. Wherefore if for any reason this adaptation should cease to exist, they lose their first meaning and accordingly must be changed.

Q. What regard have Modernists for dogmatic formulas?

A. Since the character and lot of dogmatic formulas are so precarious, there is no room for surprise that Modernists regard them so lightly and in such open disrespect.

Q. What attitude do the Modernists take toward the Church in the matter of dogmatic formulas?

A. They audaciously charge the Church both with taking the wrong road from inability to distinguish the religious and moral sense of formulas from their surface meaning, and with clinging tenaciously and vainly to meaningless formulas whilst religion is allowed to go to ruin.

Q. What must be our final judgment on the Modernists' doctrine of dogmatic truth?

A. Blind that they are, and *leaders of the blind,* inflated with a boastful science, they have reached that pitch of folly where they pervert the eternal concept of truth and the true nature of the religious sentiment; with that new system of theirs *they are seen to be under the sway of a blind and unchecked passion for novelty, thinking not at all of finding some solid foundation of truth, but despising the holy and apostolic traditions, they embrace other vain, futile, uncertain doctrines, condemned by the Church, on which, in the height of their vanity, they think they can rest and maintain truth itself.* (Greg. xvi., Encyc. VII. k. Jul., 1834.)

CHAPTER II.

The Modernist as Believer.

§1. *Religious Experience.*

Q. Thus far we have considered the Modernist as "philosopher." How shall we distinguish the Modernist as believer from the Modernist as "philosopher?"

A. If we proceed to consider him as believer, seeking to know how the believer, according to Modernism, is differentiated from the philosopher, it must be observed that although the philosopher recognizes as the object of faith the *divine reality,* still this reality is not to be found but in the heart of the believer, as being an object of sentiment and affirmation; and therefore confined within the sphere of phenomena; but as to whether it exists outside that sentiment and affirmation is a matter which in no way concerns the philosopher. For the Modernist believer, on the contrary, it is an established and certain fact that the divine reality does really exist in itself and quite independently of the person who believes in it.

Q. If, then, you ask "on what foundation this assertion of the believer rests," what do the Modernists reply?

A. In the *experience of the individual.*

Q. How do the Modernists differ from the "rationalists?"

A. On this head the Modernists differ from the *rationalists* only to fall into the opinion of the Protestants and pseudo-Mystics.

Q. How do the Modernists explain their teaching that through individual experience they attain personal certitude of the existence of God?

A. This is their manner of putting the question: In *the religious sentiment* one must recognize a kind of intuition of the heart which puts man in immediate contact with the very reality of God, and infuses such a persuasion of God's existence and His action both within and without man as to excel greatly any scientific conviction.

Q. They arrive at immediate contact without any intermediary. What certitude, then, do they claim to reach by this intuition of the heart?

A. They assert the existence of a real experience, and one of a kind that surpasses all rational experience.

Q. This being the case, whence comes it that some men deny the existence of God?

A. If this experience is denied by some, like the rationalists, it arises from the fact that such persons are unwilling to put themselves in the moral state which is necessary to produce it.

Q. Is it this "individual experience" which makes the believer?

A. It is this *experience* which, when a person acquires it, makes him properly and truly a believer.

Q. Is not all this contrary to the Catholic teaching?

A. How far off we are here from Catholic teaching we have already seen in the decree of the Vatican Council. We shall see later how, with such theories, added to the other errors already mentioned, the way is opened wide for atheism.

Q. To be consistent does it not seem from these principles, that the Modernists should advocate the truth of every religion?

A. Here it is well to note that, given this doctrine of *experience* united with the other doctrine of *symbolism*, every religion, even that of paganism, must be held to be true. What is to prevent such experiences from being met with in *every religion?* . In fact that they are to be found is asserted by not a few. And with what right will Modernists deny the truth of an experience affirmed by a follower of Islam?

Q. In virtue of what principle do they attribute to Catholics alone the monopoly of " true experiences?"

A. With what right can they claim true experiences for Catholics alone? Modernists do not deny, but actually admit, some confusedly, others in the most open manner, that *all religions are true.*

Q. Draw a strict conclusion from the Modernist principles?

A. That they can not feel otherwise is clear. For on what ground, according to their theories, could falsity be predicated of any religion whatsoever? It must be certainly on one of these two: either on account of the falsity of the religious sentiment or on account of the falsity of the formula pronounced by the mind. Now the *religious sentiment,* although it may be more perfect or less perfect, is always one and the same; and the intellectual formula, in order to be true, has but to respond to the *religious sentiment* and to the believer, whatever be the intellectual capacity of the latter.

Q. Do not the Modernists insist on the superiority of the Catholic religion?

A. In the conflict between different religions, *the most that Modernists can maintain is that the Catholic religion has more truths,* because it is more living, and that it deserves with more reason the name of Christian, because it corresponds more fully with the origins of Christianity. That these consequences flow from the premises will not seem unnatural to anybody.

Q. Do not Catholics and even priests act as if they admitted such a monstrous doctrine?

A. What is amazing is that there are Catholics and priests who, We would fain believe, abhor such enormities, yet act as if they fully approved of them. For they heap such praise and bestow such public honor on the teachers of these errors as to give rise to the belief that their admiration is not meant merely for the persons, who are perhaps not devoid of a certain merit, but rather for the errors which these persons openly profess, and which they do all in their power to propagate.

§2. *Tradition.*

Q. Do the Modernists extend the principle of religious experience to Tradition?

A. This doctrine of *experience* is also, under another aspect, entirely contrary to Catholic truth. It is extended and applied to *Tradition,* as hitherto understood by the Church, and destroys it.

Q. What is Tradition, according to the Modernists?

A. By the Modernists Tradition is understood as a communication to others, through preaching by means of the intellectual formula, of an *original experience.*

Q. What efficacy do the Modernists attribute to the intellectual formula in its relation to preaching?

A. To this formula, in addition to its representative value, they attribute a species of suggestive efficacy.

Q. In whom does the "suggestive efficacy" act?

A. It acts both in the person who believes to stimulate the religious sentiment should it happen to have grown sluggish, and to renew the experience once required, and in those who do not yet believe, to awake for the first time the religious *sentiment* in them and to produce the *experience.*

Q. Does religious experience propagate Tradition?

A. In this way is religious experience propagated among the peoples; and not merely among contemporaries by preaching, but among future generations both by books and by oral transmission from one to another. Sometimes this communication of religious experience takes root and thrives, at other times it withers at once and dies.

Q. What is the "proof of truth" for Tradition among the Modernists?

A. For the Modernists *to live* is a proof of truth, since for them life and truth are one and the same thing.

Q. What conclusion are we to draw in regard to existing religions?

A. Hence again it is given to us to infer that all existing religions are equally true, for otherwise they *would not live.*

§3. *Relation between Faith and Science.*

Q. Can we now give an idea of the relations between science—including also history under this head —and faith?

A. Having reached this point we have sufficient material in hand to enable us to see the relations which Modernists establish between faith and science, including history, also under the name of science.

Q. What distinction do the Modernists place between the object of faith and the object of science?

A. In the first place it is to be held that the object of the one is quite extraneous to and separate from the object of the other. For faith occupies itself solely with something which science declares to be *unknowable* for it. Hence each has a separate field assigned to it: science is entirely concerned with the reality of phenomena, into which faith does not enter at all; faith, on the contrary, concerns itself with the divine reality which is entirely unknown to science.

Q. Is a conflict between science and faith possible for the Modernist?

A. The conclusion is reached that there can *never be any dissension* between faith and science, for if each keeps on its own ground they can never meet, and therefore never be in contradiction.

Q. And if it be objected that in the visible world there are some things which appertain to faith, such as the human life of Christ, what do the Modernists answer?

A. The Modernists reply by denying this.

Q. How can they deny it?

A. They say: Though such things come within the category of phenomena, still in as far as they are *lived* by faith and in the way already described have been by faith *transfigured* and *disfigured*, they have been removed from the world of sense and translated to become material for the divine.

46

Q. Hence should it be further asked whether Christ has wrought real miracles, and made real prophecies, whether He rose truly from the dead and ascended into heaven, what do the Modernists answer?

A. The answer of agnostic science will be in the negative, and the answer of faith in the affirmative.

Q. But is there not here a flagrant contradiction between faith and science?

A. No, they answer. *There will not be, on that account, any conflict between them.* For it will be denied by the philosopher as philosopher, speaking to philosophers and considering Christ only in His historical reality; and it will be affirmed by the believer, speaking to believers, and considering the life of Christ as *lived* again by the faith and in the faith.

Q. Since science and faith thus deal with separate fields, is it not true, according to the Modernist, that one should be subjected in some way to the other?

A. It would be a great mistake to suppose that, given these theories, one is authorized to believe that faith and science are independent of each other. On the side of science the independence is indeed complete, but it is quite different with regard to faith, which is subject to science.

Q. Upon what ground is faith to be subject to science?

A. Faith is to be subject to science *not on one, but upon three grounds.*

Q. What is the first ground of subjection?

A. In the first place it must be observed that in every religious fact, when you take away the *divine reality* and the *experience* of it which the believer possesses, everything else, and especially the *religious formulas* of it, belongs to the sphere of phenomena and therefore falls under the control of science. Let the believer leave the world if he will, but so long as he remains in it he must continue, whether he like it or not, to be subject to the laws, the observation, the judgments of science and of history.

Q. Give the second ground for subjecting faith to science, according to the Modernists?

A. When it is said that God is the object of faith alone, the statement refers only to the *divine reality,* not to the *idea* of God. The latter also is subject to science which, while it philosophizes in what is called the logical order, soars also to the absolute and the ideal. It is therefore the right of philosophy and of science to form conclusions concerning the idea of God, to direct it in its evolution and to purify it of any extraneous elements which may become confused with it.

Q. What is the third ground?

A. Man does not suffer a dualism to exist in him, and the believer therefore feels within him an impelling need so to harmonize faith with science, that it may never oppose the general conception which science sets forth concerning the universe.

Q. The Modernist notion, therefore, is the subjection of faith to science, is it not?

A. It is evident that science is to be entirely independent of faith, while on the other hand, and notwithstanding that they are supposed to be strangers to each other, faith is made subject to science.

Q. How have Pius IX and Gregory IX stigmatized doctrines of this kind?

A. All this is in formal opposition with the teachings of Our Predecessor, Pius IX, where he lays it down that: *In matters of religion it is the duty of philosophy not to command but to serve, not to prescribe what is to be believed, but to embrace what is to be believed with reasonable obedience, not to scrutinize the depths of the mysteries of God, but to venerate them devoutly and humbly.* (Brev. ad Ep. Wratislav., 15 June, 1857.)

The Modernists completely invert the parts, and to them may be applied the words of another Predecessor of Ours, Gregory IX, addressed to some theologians of his time: *Some among you, inflated like bladders with the spirit of vanity, strive by profane novelties to cross the boundaries fixed by the Fathers, twisting the sense of the heavenly pages . . . to the philosophical teaching of the rationals, not for the profit of their hearers but to make a show of science . . . these, seduced by strange and eccentric doctrines, make the head of the tail and force the queen to serve the servant.* (Ep. ad Magistros theol. Paris, non Jul., 1223.)

§4. *Practical Consequences.*

Q. Is the conduct of Modernist Catholics in conformity with their principles?

A. This becomes clear to anybody who studies the conduct of Modernists, which is in perfect harmony with their teachings. In their writings and addresses they seem not unfrequently to advocate now one doctrine, now another, so that one would be disposed to regard them as vague and doubtful. But there is a reason for this, and it is to be found in their ideas as to the mutual separation of science and faith. Hence in their books you find some things which might well be expressed by a Catholic, but in the next page you find other things which might have been dictated by a rationalist.

Q. Do they not take a double attitude in historical matters?

A. Yes. When they write history they make no mention of the divinity of Christ, but when they are in the pulpit they profess it clearly; again, when they write history they pay no heed to the Fathers and the Councils, but when they catechize the people, they cite them respectfully.

Q. What method do they pursue in exegesis?

A. In the same way they draw their distinctions between theological and pastoral exegesis and scientific and historical exegesis.

Q. And in other scientific matters, how do they proceed?

A. Acting on the principle that science in no way depends upon faith, when they treat of philosophy, history, criticism, *feeling no horror at treading in the footsteps of Luther* (1) they are wont to display a certain contempt for Catholic doctrines, for the Holy Fathers, for the Ecumenical Councils, for the ecclesiastical magisterium; and should they be rebuked for this, they complain that they are being deprived of their liberty.

Q. What is the attitude of Modernist Catholics toward the magisterium of the Church?

A. Guided by the theory that faith must be subject to science, they continuously and openly criticise the Church because of her sheer obstinacy in refusing to submit and accommodate her dogmas to the opinions of philosophy.

Q. What do they endeavor to introduce into Catholic theology?

A. Having blotted out the old theology they endeavor to introduce a new theology which shall follow the vagaries of their philosophers.

---

(1) Prop. 29 damn. a Leone X. Bull. *Exsurge Domine* 16 maii 1520. *Via nobis facta est enervandi auctoritatem Conciliorum, et libere contradicendi eorum gestis, et iudicandi eorum decreta, et confidenter confitendi quidquid verum videtur, sive probatum fuerit, sive reprobatum a quocumque Concilio.*

CHAPTER III.

THE MODERNIST AS THEOLOGIAN.

§1. *Immanence and Theological Symbolism.*

Q. Thus, the road is open for us to study the Modernist in the theological arena. Give the system of the Modernist theologian?

A. It is a difficult task, yet one that may be disposed of briefly.

Q. What is the end in view for the Modernist?

A. The end to be attained is the *conciliation of faith with science,* always saving the primacy of science over faith.

Q. What is his method?

A. In this branch the *Modernist theologian* avails himself of exactly the same principles which we have seen employed by the Modernist philosopher, and applies them to the believer: the principles of *immanence* and *symbolism.*

Q. What is his mode of procedure?

A. The process is an extremely simple one. The philosopher has declared: *The principle of faith is immanent;* the believer has added: *This principle is God;* and the theologian draws the conclusion: *God is immanent in man.* Thus we have *theological immanence.* So, too, the philosopher regards as certain that the *representations of the object of faith are merely symbolical;* the believer has affirmed that *the object of faith is God in Himself;* and the theologian proceeds to affirm that: *The representations of the divine reality are symbolical.* And thus we have *theological symbolism.*

Q. What must be our judgment on immanence and theological symbolism?

A. They are truly enormous errors both, the pernicious character of which will be clearly seen from an examination of their consequences.

Q. Mention some of the consequences of theological symbolism?

A. To begin with *symbolism,* since symbols are but *symbols* in regard to their objects and only instruments in regard to the believer, it is necessary first of all, according to the teachings of the Modernists, that the believer do not lay too much stress on the formula, but avail himself of it only with the scope of uniting himself to the absolute truth which the formula at once reveals and conceals, that is to say, endeavors to express but without succeeding in doing so.

Q. Are there any further consequences?

A. Yes. They would also have the believer avail himself of the formulas only in as far as they are useful to him, for they are given to be a help and not a hindrance.

Q. Is the believer to use the formulas according to his own desires?

A. Yes, replies the Modernist, but with proper regard, however, for the social respect due to formulas which the public magisterium has deemed suitable for expressing the common consciousness until such time as the same magisterium provide otherwise.

Q. What do the Modernists really mean by theological immanence?

A. Concerning *immanence* it is not easy to determine what Modernists mean by it, for their own opinions on the subject vary.

Q. Give the different opinions of the Modernists, and their consequences on theological immanence?

A. Some understand it in the sense that God working in man is more intimately present in him than man is in even himself, and this conception, if properly understood, is free from reproach. Others hold that the divine action is one with the action of nature, as the action of the first cause is one with the action of the secondary cause, and this would destroy the supernatural order. Others, finally, explain it in a way which savors of Pantheism and this, in truth, is the sense which tallies best with the rest of their doctrines.

§2. *Divine Permanence.*

Q. What other Modernist opinion is closely allied with the principle of immanence?

A. With this principle of *immanence* is connected another which may be called the principle of *divine permanence.*

Q. In what does this principle differ from the former?

A. It differs from the first in much the same way as the *private experience* differs from the *experience transmitted by Tradition.*

Q. This is not very clearly stated. Explain the doctrine by an example?

A. An example will illustrate what is meant, and this is offered by the Church and the Sacraments.

Q. What do the Modernists say of the institution of the Church and of the Sacraments?

A. The Church and the Sacraments, they say, are *not to be regarded* as *having been instituted by Christ* Himself.

Q. How can the institution of the Sacraments and of the Church by Jesus Christ Himself be in contradiction to Modernist principles?

A. This is forbidden by Agnosticism, which sees in Christ nothing more than a man whose religious consciousness has been, like that of all men, formed by degrees; it is also forbidden by the law of immanence, which rejects what they call external *application;* it is further forbidden by the law of evolution, which requires for the development of the germs a certain time and a certain series of circumstances; it is, finally, forbidden by history, which shows that such in fact has been the course of things.

Q. Were not the Sacraments and the Church then instituted by Christ?

A. It is to be held that both Church and Sacraments have been founded *mediately* by Christ.

Q. How do the Modernist theologians endeavor to prove this divine origin of the Church and of the Sacraments?

A. In this way: All Christian consciences were, they affirm, in a manner virtually included in the conscience of Christ as the plant is included in the seed. But as the shoots live the life of the seed, so, too, all Christians are to be said to live the life of Christ. But the life of Christ is according to faith, and so, too, is the life of Christians. And since this life produced, in the course of ages, both the Church and the Sacraments, it is quite right to say that their origin is from Christ, and is divine.

Q. Do not the Modernists follow the same method in proving the divinity of the Holy Scriptures and the dogmas?

A. In the same way they prove that the Scriptures and the dogmas are divine.

Q. Does this constitute the entire theology of the Modernists?

A. The Modernistic theology may thus be said to be complete. No great thing, in truth, but more than enough for the theologian who professes that the conclusions of science must always, and in all things, be respected. The application of these theories to the other points anybody may easily make for himself.

CHAPTER IV.

The Religious Philosophy of the Modernists (Continued) : "Shoots" of the Faith.

§1. Dogma.

Q. Thus far you have spoken of the origin and nature of faith. Among the Modernists, has not the faith many "shoots"?

A. The faith has *many shoots,* and chief among them are the Church, dogma, worship, the Books which we call Sacred.

Q. Tell us what the Modernists teach about these "shoots?"

A. To begin with dogma, we have already indicated its nature and origin.

Q. How is dogma "born," according to the Modernist theology?

A. Dogma is *born of a species of impulse or necessity,* by virtue of which the believer is constrained to elaborate his religious thought so as to render it clearer for himself and others.

Q. In what does this "elaboration of religious thought" consist?

A. This elaboration consists entirely in the process of penetrating and refining the primitive *formula.*

Q. Is this elaboration of rational or logical development?

A. It is not, they say, in itself, according to logical development. It develops as required by circumstances, or *vitally*, as the Modernists more abstrusely put it.

Q. What, according to the Modernists, is produced by this elaboration of religious thought?

A. Around the *primitive* formula, *secondary* formulas gradually continue to be formed, and these subsequently grouped into bodies of doctrine, or into doctrinal constructions as they prefer to call them, and further sanctioned by the public magisterium as responding to the common consciousness, are called dogma.

Q. Do the Modernists distinguish dogma from the speculations of theologians?

A. Yes. Dogma is to be carefully distinguished from the speculations of theologians.

Q. Of what utility, then, are the speculations of theologians?

A. Although not alive with the life of dogma, they are not without their utility as serving to harmonize religion with science and remove opposition between the two, in such a way as to throw light from without on religion, and, it may be, even to prepare the matter for future dogma.

§2. *Worship.*

Q. What is the Modernist's theological doctrine on worship and the Sacraments?

A. Concerning worship there would not be much to be said, were it not that under this head are comprised the Sacraments, concerning which the Modernists fall into the gravest errors.

Q. According to the Modernists, of what are the Sacraments and worship the resultant?

A. For them the Sacraments are the resultant of a double need—for, as we have seen, everything in their system is explained by inner impulses or necessities.

Q. Explain this "double need" of which the Modernist theologians speak?

A. In the present case, the *first need* is that of giving some manifestation to religion; the *second* is that of propagating it, which could not be done without some sensible form and consecrating acts, and these are called Sacraments.

Q. What, according to the Modernists, are the Sacraments? To what may they be compared?

A. For the Modernists the *Sacraments are mere symbols* or signs, though not devoid of a certain efficacy—an efficacy, they tell us, like that of certain phrases vulgarly described as having " *caught on,*" inasmuch as they have become the vehicle for the diffusion of certain great ideas which strike the public mind. What the phrases are to the ideas, that the Sacraments are to the religious sentiment—that and nothing more.

Q. To be consistent, should not the Modernists add something further?

A. The Modernists would be speaking more clearly were they to affirm that the Sacraments are instituted solely to *foster the faith*—but this is condemned by the Council of Trent: *If any one say that these Sacraments are instituted solely to foster the faith, let him be anathema.* (Sess. VII. de Sacramentis in genere, can. 5.)

§3. *The Sacred Books—Inspiration.*

Q. What are the Sacred Books for the Modernist theologian, and how may they be described?

A. We have already touched upon the nature and origin of the Sacred Books. According to the principles of the Modernists they may be rightly described as a *collection of experiences,* not indeed of the kind that may come to anybody, but those extraordinary and striking ones which have happened in any religion.

Q. Does this definition also embrace our Sacred Books?

A. This is precisely what they teach about our books of the Old and New Testaments.

Q. Experience deals entirely with the present. The Sacred Books, on the other hand, contain histories of the past and prophecies of the future. How can the Modernists call them records of experience?

A. To suit their own theories they note with remarkable ingenuity that, although experience is something belonging to the present, still it may derive its material from the past and the future alike, inasmuch as the believer by memory *lives* the past over again after the manner of *the present,* and lives the future already by anticipation. This explains how it is that the historical and apocalyptical books are included among the Sacred Writings.

Q. Are not the Sacred Books the Word of God?

A. God does indeed speak in these books—through the medium of the believer, but only, according to Modernistic theology, by vital *immanence* and *permanence.*

Q. What is inspiration, according to the Modernists?

A. Inspiration, they reply, is distinguished only by its vehemence from that impulse which stimulates the believer to reveal the faith that is in him by words or writing. It is something like what happens in poetical inspiration, of which it has been said: There is a God in us, and when He stirreth He sets us afire. And it is precisely in this sense that God is said to be the origin of the inspiration of the Sacred Books.

Q. Do they admit that the inspiration of the Sacred Books is "universal?" Give the Catholic view on this subject?

A. The Modernists affirm, too, that there is nothing in these books which is not inspired. In this respect some might be disposed to consider them as more orthodox than certain other moderns who somewhat restrict inspiration, as, for instance, in what have been put forward as *tacit citations.* But it is all mere juggling of words. For if we take the Bible, according to the tenets of Agnosticism, to be a human work, made by men for men, but allowing the theologian to proclaim that it is divine by immanence, what room is there left in it for inspiration? General inspiration in the Modernist sense it is easy to find, but of inspiration in the Catholic sense there is not a trace.

§4. *The Church: Its Origin, Nature, and Rights.*

Q. We come now to the Church. What do the Modernist theologians think of the Church?

A. A wider field for comment is opened when you come to treat of the vagaries devised by the Modernist schools concerning the Church.

Q. What is the Modernist doctrine on the origin of the Church?

A. You must start with the supposition that the Church has its birth in a double need, the need of the individual believer, especially if he has had some original and special experience, to communicate his faith to others, and the need of the mass, when the faith has become common to many, to form itself into a society and to guard, increase, and propagate the common good.

Q. What, then, is the Church?

A. It is the product of the *collective conscience,* that is to say, of the society of individual consciences which by virtue of the principle of *vital permanence,* all depend on one first believer, who for Catholics is Christ.

Q. Whence, according to the Modernist theologians, comes the disciplinary, doctrinal, and liturgical authority in the Catholic Church?

A. Every society *needs* a directing authority to guide its members toward the common end, to conserve prudently the elements of cohesion which in a religious society are doctrine and worship. Hence the triple authority in the Catholic Church, *disciplinary, dogmatic, liturgical.*

Q. From what do they gather the nature and duties of authority?

A. The nature of this authority is to be gathered from its origin, and its rights and duties from its nature.

Q. What do the Modernist theologians say of the authority of the Church in past ages?

A. In past times it was a common error that authority came to the Church from without, that is to say directly from God; and it was then rightly held to be *autocratic.*

Q. What of the authority to-day?

A. This conception has now grown obsolete. For in the same way as the Church is a vital emanation of the collectivity of consciences, so too authority emanates vitally from the Church itself.

Q. Does not the authority of the Church, according to the Modernist theologians, depend on the collective conscience?

A. Authority, therefore, like the Church, has its origin in the *religious conscience,* and, that being so, is subject to it.

Q. Should the Church disown this dependence, what, according to the Modernists, is the result?

A. Should it disown this dependence it becomes a tyranny.

Q. It is not, then, a duty on the part of the Church to shape herself to democratic forms?

A. We are living in an age when the sense of liberty has reached its fullest development, and when the public conscience has in the civil order introduced popular government. Now there are not two consciences in man, any more than there are two lives. It is for the ecclesiastical authority, therefore, *to shape itself to democratic forms,* unless it wishes to provoke and foment an intestine conflict in the consciences of mankind.

Q. If the Church does not show herself pliant toward this doctrine of the Modernists, what will be the penalty for the Church and religion?

A. The penalty of refusal is *disaster.* For it is madness to think that the sentiment of liberty, as it is now spread abroad, can surrender. Were it forcibly confined and held in bonds, terrible would be its outburst, sweeping away at once both Church and religion.

Q. What, finally, is the one great anxiety of the Modernists?

A. Their one great anxiety is, in consequence, to find a way of *conciliation* between the authority of the Church and the liberty of believers.

§5. *Church and State.*

Q. Must not the Church come to an amicable arrangement with civil societies?

A. It is not with its own members alone that the *Church must come to an amicable arrangement*—besides its relations with those within, it has others outside. The Church does not occupy the world all by itself; there are other societies in the world, with which it must necessarily have contact and relations.

Q. What are the rights and duties of the Church toward civil societies?

A. The rights and duties of the Church toward civil societies must, therefore, be determined, and determined, of course, by its own nature as it has been already described.

Q. What rules are to be applied to the relations of Church and State?

A. The *rules to be applied* in this matter are those which have been laid down for science and faith, though in the latter case the question is one of *objects* while here we have one of *ends*. In the same way, then, as faith and science are strangers to each other by reason of the diversity of their objects, Church and State are strangers by reason of the diversity of their ends, that of the Church being spiritual, while that of the State is temporal.

Q. Why, according to the Modernists, was there formerly attributed to the Church an authority which is denied her to-day?

A. Formerly it was possible to subordinate the temporal to the spiritual and to speak of some questions as *mixed,* allowing to the Church the position of queen and mistress in all such, because the Church was then regarded as having been instituted immediately by God as the author of the supernatural order. But this doctrine is to-day repudiated alike by philosophy and history.

Q. Do the Modernists demand the separation of Church and State?

A. The State must, therefore, be separated from the Church, and the Catholic from the citizen.

Q. Since the Catholic is at the same time a citizen, what should be his line of conduct, according to the Modernists?

A. Every Catholic, from the fact that he is also a citizen, has the right and the duty to work for the common good in the way he thinks best, without troubling himself about the authority of the Church, without paying any heed to its wishes, its counsels, its orders—nay, even in spite of its reprimands.

Q. Has the Church, then, no right to prescribe a line of conduct for the Catholic citizen?

A. To trace out and prescribe for the citizen any line of conduct, on any pretext whatsoever, is to be guilty of an abuse of ecclesiastical authority.

Q. Should the Church intervene, is this, according to the Modernists, an abuse of authority?

A. Yes, it is an *abuse* against which one is bound to act with all one's might.

Q. Have not these principles been already condemned by the Church?

A. The principles from which these doctrines spring have been solemnly condemned by our predecessor Pius VI in his Constitution *Auctorem fidei.*(1)

Q. Are the Modernists satisfied with demanding the separation of Church and State?

A. It is not enough for the Modernist school that

---

(1) Prop. 2. *Propositio, quae statuit, potestatem a Deo datam Ecclesiae ut communicaretur Pastoribus, qui sunt eius ministri pro salute animarum; sic intellecta, ut a communitate fidelium in Pastores derivetur ecclesiastici ministerii ac regiminis potestas: haeretica.*—Prop. 3. *Insuper, quae statuit Romanum Pontificem esse caput ministeriale; sic explicata ut Romanus Pontifex non a Christo in persona beati Petri, sed ab Ecclesia potestatem ministerii accipiat, qua velut Petri successor, verus Christi vicarius ac totius Ecclesiae caput pollet in universa Ecclesia: haeretica.*

the State should be separated from the Church. For as faith is to be subordinated to science, as far as *phenomenal elements* are concerned, so, too, in temporal matters, the Church must be subject to the State.

Q. Have Modernists really the effrontery to teach this?

A. They do not say this *openly as yet*—but they will say it when they wish to be logical on this head.

Q. What pernicious results will follow from these Modernist principles?

A. Given the principle that in temporal matters the State possesses absolute mastery, it will follow that when the believer, not fully satisfied with his merely internal acts of religion, proceeds to external acts, such for instance as the administration or reception of the Sacraments, these will fall under the control of the State. What will then become of ecclesiastical authority, which can only be exercised by external acts? Obviously it will be completely under the dominion of the State.

Q. But does it not seem that, to liberate one's self from this dominion of the State—if the Modernists prevail—it will be impossible to practise external religions or even to maintain any religious society?

A. It is this inevitable consequence which impels many among liberal Protestants to reject all external worship, nay, all external religious community, and makes them advocate what they call *individual* religion.

Q. Since the Modernists have not yet gone so far, how are they preparing minds and what have they to say of the disciplinary authority of the Church?

A. If the Modernists have not yet reached this point, they do ask the Church in the meanwhile to be good enough to follow spontaneously where they lead her and adapt herself to the civil forms in vogue. Such are their ideas about *disciplinary* authority.

Q. What are their ideas on doctrinal authority?

A. Far more advanced and far more pernicious are their teachings on *doctrinal* and *dogmatic* authority.

Q. Give their conception of the magisterium of the Church?

A. This is their conception of the *magisterium of the Church:* No religious society, they say, can be a real unit unless the religious conscience of its members be one, and one also the formula which they adopt. But this double unity requires a kind of common mind whose office is to find and determine the formula that corresponds best with the common conscience, and it must have, moreover, an authority sufficient to enable it to impose on the community the formula which has been decided upon. From the combination and, as it were, fusion of these two elements, the common mind which draws up the formula and the authority which imposes it, arises, according to the Modernists, the notion of the ecclesiastical magisterium.

Q. So this is pure democracy! Does it not subordi-

nate doctrinal authority to the judgment of the people?

A. As this magisterium springs, in its last analysis, from the individual consciences, and possesses its mandate of public utility for their benefit, it follows that the ecclesiastical magisterium must be subordinate to them, and should therefore take democratic forms.

Q. Do not the Modernist theologians accuse the magisterium of the Church of abuse?

A. Yes. They say to prevent individual consciences from revealing freely and openly the impulses they feel, to hinder criticism from impelling dogmas toward their necessary evolutions—this is not a legitimate use, but an abuse of a power given for the public utility.

Q. In that measure of authority which the Modernists concede, is the Church supreme?

A. A due method and measure must be observed in the exercise of authority. To condemn and prescribe a work without the knowledge of the author, without hearing his explanations, without discussion, assuredly savors of tyranny.

Q. What is the cry of the Modernists?

A. A way must be found to save the full rights of authority on the one hand and of liberty on the other.

Q. And meanwhile, what course is the Modernist to pursue?

A. In the meanwhile the proper course for the Catholic will be to proclaim publicly his profound respect for authority—and continue to follow his own bent.

Q. Although rebels, do the Modernist theologians grant to the Church a right to solemn worship and external pomp?

A. Their general directions for the Church may be put in this way: Since the end of the Church is entirely spiritual, the religious authority should strip itself of all that external pomp which adorns it in the eyes of the public. And here they forget that while religion is essentially for the soul, it is not exclusively for the soul, and that the honor paid to authority is reflected back on Jesus Christ who instituted it.

§6. *Evolution.*

Q. Have we finished the entire doctrine of the Modernist theologians?

A. To finish with this whole question of faith and its shoots, it remains to be seen what the Modernists have to say about their *development*.

Q. How do they arrive at the chief of their doctrines?

A. First of all they lay down the general principle that in a living religion everything is subject to change, and must in fact change, and in this way they pass to what may be said to be, among the chief of their doctrines, that of *evolution*.

Q. According to the Modernists, what theological matters are subject to evolution?

A. To the laws of evolution everything is subject—dogma, Church, worship, the Books we revere as Sacred, even faith itself, and the penalty of disobedience is death.

Q. Is this, in truth, their general principle?

A. The enunciation of this principle will not astonish anybody who bears in mind what the Modernists have had to say about each of these subjects.

Q. Having laid down this law, how do the Modernists put it in action? What was the primitive form of faith?

A. Having laid down this law of evolution, the Modernists themselves teach us how it works out. And first with regard to faith. The primitive form of faith, they tell us, was *rudimentary and common to all men* alike, for it had its origin in human nature and human life.

Q. How, in the Modernist system, has faith progressed?

A. Vital evolution brought with it *progress,* not by the accretion of new and purely adventitious forms from without, but by an increasing penetration of the religious sentiment in the conscience.

Q. What was the double character of this progress of faith?

A. This progress was of two kinds: *negative,* by the elimination of all foreign elements, such, for example, as the sentiment of family or nationality; and *positive,* by that intellectual and moral refining of man, by means of which the idea was enlarged and enlightened while the religious sentiment became more elevated and more intense.

§7. *Causes of Evolution—Conserving and Progressive Force.*

Q. What causes are to be assigned for this progress of faith?

A. For the progress of faith no other causes are to be assigned than those which are adduced to explain its origin. But to them must be added those *religious geniuses* whom we call prophets, and of whom Christ was the greatest.

Q. How do the Modernists conceive that the religious geniuses aided the progress of faith?

A. They aided the progress of faith both because in their lives and their words there was something mysterious which faith attributed to the divinity, and because it fell to their lot to have new and original experiences fully in harmony with the needs of their time.

Q. To what do the Modernists chiefly attribute progress of faith?

A. The *progress of dogma* is due chiefly to the obstacles which faith has to surmount, to the enemies it has to vanquish, to the contradictions it has to repel. Add to this a perpetual striving to penetrate ever more profoundly its own mysteries.

Q. Give as an example of this, the Modernists' view on the divinity of Christ?

A. To omit other examples, it has happened in the case of Christ: in Him that divine something which faith admitted in Him expanded in such a way that He was at last held to be God.

Q. What is the chief stimulus in the domain of worship?

A. The chief stimulus of evolution in the domain of worship consists in the *need of adapting* itself to the uses and customs of peoples, as well as the need of availing itself of the value which certain acts have acquired by long usage.

Q. What is the principal factor in the evolution of the Church?

A. Evolution in the Church itself is fed by the need of accommodating itself to historical conditions, and of harmonizing itself with existing forms of society.

Q. Such is religious evolution in detail. What is the " essential root of the Modernist system?"

A. Here, before proceeding further, we would have you note well this whole theory of *necessities and needs,* for it is at the root of the entire system of the Modernists, and it is upon it that they will erect that famous method of theirs called the historical.

Q. Have we in this theory of necessities and needs, the entire system of the Modernists on evolution?

A. Still continuing the consideration of the evolution of doctrine, it is to be noted that evolution is due, no doubt, to those stimulants styled needs, but, if left to their action alone, it would run a great risk of bursting the bounds of Tradition, and thus, turned aside from its primitive vital principle, would lead to ruin instead of progress.

Q. What must we further add, in order to complete the thought of the Modernists?

A. Studying more closely the ideas of the Modernists, evolution is described as resulting from the conflict of two forces, one of them tending toward progress, the other toward conservation.

Q. What is this conserving force in the Church?

A. The conserving force in the Church is Tradition, and Tradition is represented by religious authority.

Q. How does the religious authority represent the conserving force?

A. Religious authority represents this conserving force both by right and in fact, for by right it is in the very nature of authority to protect Tradition; and in fact, for authority, raised as it is above the contingencies of life, feels hardly, or not at all, the spurs of progress.

Q. Where shall we find this conserving force?

A. The progressive force, on the contrary, which responds to the inner needs lies *in the individual consciences* and ferments there—especially in such of them as are in most intimate contact with life.

Q. Do not the Modernists place the progressive force outside the ranks of the hierarchy?

A. Note here the appearance already of that most pernicious doctrine which would make of the laity a factor of progress in the Church.

Q. By what combination of the conserving force and of the progressive force do the Modernists advance " modifications and progress " in the Church?

A. It is by a species of compromise between the forces of conservation and of progress, that is to say between authority and individual consciences, that changes and advances take place. The individual consciences of some of them act on the collective conscience, which brings pressure to bear on the depositaries of authority, until the latter consent to a compromise, and, the pact being made, authority sees to its maintenance.

§8. *Practical Consequences.*

Q. When reprimanded or punished by the religious authority, what do the Modernists express?

A. With all this in mind, one understands how it is that the Modernists express *astonishment* when they are reprimanded or punished. What is imputed to them as a fault they regard as a sacred duty. Being in intimate contact with consciences they know better than anybody else, and certainly better than the ecclesiastical authority, what needs exist—nay, they embody them, so to speak, in themselves. Having a voice and a pen, they use both publicly, for this is their duty. Let authority rebuke them as much as it pleases—they have their own consciences on their side and an intimate experience which tells them with certainty that what they deserve is not blame but praise.

Q. What attitude do those Modernists who are reprimanded by the Church take?

A. They reflect that, after all, there is no progress without a battle and no battle without its victim, and victims they are willing to be, like the prophets and Christ Himself. They have no bitterness in their hearts against the authority which uses them roughly, for, after all, it is only doing its duty as authority. Their sole grief is that it remains deaf to their warnings, because delay multiplies the obstacles which impede the progress of souls.

Q. What hope do they cherish?

A. They cherish the hope that the hour will most surely come when there will be no further chance for tergiversation, for if the laws of evolution may be checked for a while, they can not be ultimately destroyed.

Q. At least they do not continue in their ways?

A. They go their way, reprimands and condemnations notwithstanding, masking an incredible audacity under a mock semblance of humility. While they make a show of bowing their heads, their hands and minds are more intent than ever on carrying out their purposes.

Q. Why, then, do the Modernists pretend to submit? Why do they not rather leave the Church as heretics?

A. This policy they follow willingly and wittingly, both because it is part of their system that authority is to be stimulated but not dethroned, and because it is necessary for them to remain within the ranks of the Church in order that they may gradually transform the collective conscience.

Q. Their idea is that they may gradually transform the collective conscience? Should they not, according to their principles, submit to this collective conscience?

A. They should, but remaining as they do within the Church, they unconsciously avow that the common conscience is not with them, and that they have no right to claim to be its interpreters.

§9. *Condemnation.*

Q. What should be our conclusion regarding the doctrines of the Modernists?

A. This should be our conclusion: for the Modernists, both as authors and propagandists, there is to be nothing stable, nothing immutable in the Church.

Q. Had they not precursors in their doctrines?

A. Nor indeed are they without precursors in their doctrines, for it was of these that Our Predecessor

Pius IX wrote: *These enemies of divine revelation extol human progress to the skies, and with rash and sacrilegious daring would have it introduced into the Catholic religion as if this religion were not the work of God but of man, or some kind of philosophical discovery susceptible of perfection by human efforts.* (Encycl. *Qui pluri*, 9 Nov., 1846.)

Q. Do the Modernists give us a really new doctrine on revelation and dogma? Has not their system been already condemned?

A. On the subject of revelation and dogma in particular, the doctrine of the Modernists offers nothing new—we find it condemned in the Syllabus of Pius IX, where it is enunciated in these terms: *Divine revelation is imperfect, and therefore subject to continual and indefinite progress, corresponding with the progress of human reason* (Syll. Prop. 5), and condemned still more solemnly in the Vatican Council: *The doctrine of the faith which God has revealed has not been proposed to human intelligences to be perfected by them as if it were a philosophical system, but as a divine deposit entrusted to the Spouse of Christ to be faithfully guarded and infallibly interpreted. Hence the sense, too, of the sacred dogmas is that which our Holy Mother the Church has once declared, nor is this sense ever to be abandoned on plea or pretext of a more profound comprehension of the truth.* (Const. *Dei Filius*, cap. iv.)

Q.   Does the Church intend to impede the development of knowledge, even in matters concerning the faith?

A.   Nor is the development of our knowledge, even concerning the faith, impeded by this pronouncement —on the contrary it is aided and promoted.   For the same Council continues: *Let intelligence and science and wisdom, therefore, increase and progress abundantly and vigorously in individuals and in the mass, in the believer and in the whole Church, throughout the ages and the centuries—but only in its own kind, that is, according to the same dogma, the same sense, the same acceptation. (Loc. cit.)*

CHAPTER V.

THE MODERNIST AS HISTORIAN AND CRITIC.

§1. *Application of Agnosticism.*

Q. Having studied the Modernist as philosopher, believer, and theologian, what remains?

A. It now remains for us to consider him as historian, critic, apologist, reformer.

Q. What do certain Modernists, who are devoted to historical studies, fear?

A. Some Modernists, devoted to historical studies, seem to be greatly afraid of being taken for philosophers.

Q. What do they say of their knowledge of philosophy?

A. About philosophy, they tell you, they know nothing whatever.

Q. Is this affectation of ignorance sincere?

A. No, for in this they display remarkable astuteness.

Q. Why, then, do the Modernist historians profess ignorance of philosophy?

A. They are particularly anxious not to be suspected of being prejudiced in favor of philosophical theories which would lay them open to the charge of not being *objective,* to use the word in vogue.

Q. Do not the Modernist historians allow themselves to be influenced by philosophical systems?

A. Yes. The truth is that their history and their criticism are saturated with their philosophy, and that their historico-critical conclusions are the natural fruit of their philosophical principles. This will be patent to anybody who reflects.

Q. What are the three philosophical principles from which the Modernist historians deduce their three laws of history?

A. Their three first laws are contained in those three principles of their philosophy, already dealt with: the principle of *Agnosticism,* the principle of the *transfiguration* of things by faith, and the principle which We have called of *disfiguration.*

Q. What is the historical law which, according to the Modernists, flows from the philosophic principle of Agnosticism?

A. Agnosticism tells us that history, like every other science, deals entirely with phenomena.

Q. What conclusion flows immediately from this first law of history, which has been deduced from Agnosticism?

A. The consequence is that God, and every intervention of God in human affairs, is to be relegated to the domain of faith as belonging to it alone.

Q. In history, when a double element, the divine and the human, mingles, what is the procedure of the Modernist?

A. In things where a double element, the divine and the human, mingles—in Christ, for example, or the Church, or the Sacraments, or the many other objects of the same kind—a division must be made and the human element assigned to history while the divine will go to faith.

Q. Must we not, therefore, distinguish two Christs, two Churches, etc.?

A. Yes. We have that distinction, so current among the Modernists, between the Christ of history and the Christ of faith, between the Church of history and the Church of faith, between the Sacraments of history and the Sacraments of faith, and so on.

Q. In regard to that human element, which alone Agnosticism allows us to retain for historical work, what does the second philosophical principle, or the principle of transfiguration, teach the Modernist?

A. We find that the human element itself, which the historian has to work on, as it appears in the documents, has been by faith transfigured; that is to say, raised above its historical conditions.

Q. According to this principle of transfiguration, what second law governs Modernist history?

A. It becomes necessary to eliminate also the accretions which faith has added, to assign them to faith itself, and to the history of faith.

Q. Consequently, what must the Modernist historian eliminate from the history of Jesus Christ?

A. When treating of Christ, the historian must set aside all that surpasses man in his natural condition, either according to the psychological conception of him, or according to the place and period of his existence.

Q. What third law does the Modernist derive from the philosophical principle of disfiguration?

A. By virtue of the *third principle,* even those things which are not outside the sphere of history they pass through the crucible, excluding from history and relegating to faith everything which, in their judgment, is not in harmony with what they call the *logic* of facts, and in character with the persons of whom they are predicted.

Q. Following this third law, what conclusions do the Modernists draw in regard to the words which the Evangelists attribute to our Saviour?

A. They will not allow that Christ ever uttered those things which do not seem to be within the capacity of the multitudes that listened to Him. Hence they delete from His *real* history and transfer to faith all the allegories found in His discourses.

Q. Will you tell us by what criterion the Modernists make these divisions?

A. Do you inquire as to the criterion they adopt to enable them to make these divisions? The reply is that they argue from the character of the man, from his condition of life, from his education, from the circumstances under which the facts took place.

Q. Is the criterion objective as serious historical study requires?

A. The criteria, when one considers them well, are purely *subjective*.

Q. Show that this criterion is purely subjective?

A. The Modernist method is to put themselves into the position and person of Christ, and then to attribute to Him what they would have done under like circumstances.

Q. Following the three philosophic principles which govern their history, how do the Modernists deal with Christ as God?

A. In this way, absolutely *a priori* and acting on philosophical principles which they admit they hold, but which they affect to ignore, they proclaim that Christ, according to what they call His *real* history, was not God and never did anything divine.

Q. Eliminating from the real Christ of history every divine attribute, do they leave His humanity intact?

A. No. They say that as man He did and said only what they, judging from the time in which He lived, can admit Him to have said or done.

Q. What bond of union do the Modernists find among philosophy, history, and criticism?

A. As history receives its conclusions, ready-made, from philosophy, so, too, criticism takes its own from history.

Q. How does the Modernist critic deal with the documents upon which he works?

A. The critic, on the data furnished him by the historian, makes two parts of all his documents. Those that remain after the triple elimination above described go to form the *real* history; the rest is attributed to the history of the faith or, as it is styled, to *internal* history.

Q. Are there not, then, two histories for the Modernist—the history of faith and real history?

A. The Modernists distinguish very carefully between these two kinds of history.

Q. Is the history of faith real history for the Modernists?

A. It is to be noted that they oppose the history of faith to real history precisely as real.

Q. If the history of faith is not real history, what do the Modernists say of the two Christs whom we mentioned above?

A. They hold that we have a double Christ: a real Christ, and a Christ, the one of faith, who never really existed; a Christ who has lived at a given time and in a given place, and a Christ who has never lived outside the pious meditations of the believer.

Q. Where is the Christ of faith—who is not the Christ of the Modernists—portrayed?

A. He is the Christ, for instance, whom we find in the Gospel of St. John.

*Q. What is the opinion of the Modernists on the
subject of St. John's Gospel?*

A. It is pure contemplation from beginning to end.

§2. *Application of Vital Immanence.*

*Q. Does the dominion of philosophy over history
end with criticizing the division of documents into two
parts; viz., documents which serve for the history of
faith and documents which serve for real history?*

A. The dominion of philosophy over history does
not end here.

*Q. After this Agnostic division of documents into
two parts, what other principle of Modernist philosophy steps in to govern criticism?*

A. Given that division, of which we have spoken,
of the documents into two parts, the philosopher steps
in again with his principle of *vital immanence.*

*Q. To the Modernist critic what is the importance
of the principle of vital immanence?*

A. It shows how everything in the history of the
Church is to be explained by *vital emanation.*

*Q. How can facts which are only "vital emana-
tions" be subordinated to an immanent need which
they ante-date?*

A. Since the cause or condition of every vital emanation whatsoever is to be found in some need, it follows that no fact can ante-date the need which produced

it—historically the *fact must be posterior to the need.*

Q. Armed with such a principle, how does the Modernist historian proceed in the history of the Church?

A. He goes over his documents again, whether they be found in the Sacred Books or elsewhere, draws up from them his list of the successive needs of the Church, whether relating to dogma or liturgy or other matters.

Q. What does the Modernist historian then do with his list?

A. Then he hands his list over to the critic.

Q. Reinforced by his " list " of successive needs of the Church, what labor does the critic expend, then, on the documents of the history of faith?

A. The critic takes in hand the *documents* dealing with the history of faith and distributes them, period by period, so that they correspond exactly with the lists of needs, always guided by the principle that the narration must follow the facts, as the facts follow the needs.

Q. In the Sacred Books, does it not sometimes happen that certain parts, instead of revealing a simple need, rather are themselves the creation of a need?

A. It may at times happen that some parts of the Sacred Scriptures, such as the Epistles, themselves constitute the fact created by the need.

Q. Apart from exceptions, what, in a general way,

*is the law which serves to determine the date of origin
of documents for ecclesiastical history?*

A. The rule holds that the age of any document
can only be determined by the age in which each need
has manifested itself in the Church.

§3. *Application of Evolutionism.*

Q. *After this work, which has classified the documents according to a date of origin arbitrarily determined, does not another operation follow?*

A. Another *operation* follows.

Q. *What distinction, in the eyes of the Modernist
critic, makes necessary this new operation?*

A. A distinction must be made between the beginning of a fact and its development, for what is born
one day requires time for growth.

Q. *In virtue of this distinction between the origin
of a fact and its development, what new division does
the critic introduce among his documents?*

A. The critic must once more go over his documents, ranged as they are through the different ages,
and divide them again into two parts, separating those
that regard the first stage of the facts from those that
deal with their development.

Q. *What must the critic do with documents which
deal with the development of a fact?*

A. These he must again arrange according to their
periods.

THE MODERNIST AS HISTORIAN AND CRITIC

Q. What principle, according to the Modernist philosopher, must dominate and rule history?

A. The philosopher must come in again to impose on the historian the obligation of following in all his studies the precepts and laws of evolution.

Q. How shall the Modernist historian, now armed with the law of evolution, treat the history of the Church?

A. It is next for the historian to scrutinize his documents once more, to examine carefully the circumstances and conditions affecting the Church during the different periods, the conserving force she has put forth, the needs both internal and external that have stimulated her to progress, the obstacles she has had to encounter.

Q. In a word, what does the Modernist historian seek in documents relating to the history of the Church?

A. In a word, he seeks everything that helps to determine the manner in which the laws of evolution have been fulfilled in her.

Q. After this attentive examination to discover in the history of the Church the law of her evolution, what is the office of the critic?

A. This done, he finishes his work by drawing up in its broad lines a history of the development of the facts.

Q. When he has traced out this fantastic sketch of the history of the Church, what is the last labor of the Modernist critic?

A. The critic follows and fits in the rest of the documents with this sketch; he takes up his pen, and soon the history is made complete.

Q. Now we ask here: Who is the author of this history? The historian? The critic?

A. Assuredly, neither of these, but the philosopher.

Q. Why is the philosopher the author of this history?

A. Because, from beginning to end everything in it is *a priori*.

Q. What is the character of this "a priori" method?

A. It is *a priori* in a way that reeks of heresy.

Q. Are not these historians to be pitied?

A. These men are certainly to be pitied, and of them the Apostle might well say: *They became vain in their thoughts . . . professing themselves to be wise they became fools* (Rom. i. 21, 22).

Q. But if they are to be pitied, do not these Modernist historians equally merit our indignation?

A. At the same time, they excite just indignation when they accuse the Church of torturing the texts, arranging and confusing them after its own fashion, and for the needs of its cause.

Q. Why do they accuse the Church of "torturing" texts?

A. They are accusing the Church of something for which their own conscience plainly reproaches them.

§4. Textual Criticism.

Q. If the Modernist historian has arbitrarily dismembered documents, and partitioned them throughout the centuries, according to the supposed exigencies of the law of evolution, what will be the result in regard to the Sacred Books?

A. The result of this dismembering of the Sacred Books and this partition of them throughout the centuries is naturally that the Scriptures can no longer be attributed to the authors whose names they bear.

Q. Do not our Modernist historians hesitate at this?

A. The Modernists have no hesitation in affirming commonly that these books, and especially the Pentateuch and the first three Gospels, have been gradually formed by additions to a primitive brief narration—by interpolations of theological or allegorical interpretation, by transitions, by joining different passages together.

Q. Upon what do they rely to explain the origin of the Sacred Books, granting the supposition of successive additions to an exceedingly brief primitive redaction?

A. This means, briefly, that in the Sacred Books we must admit a *vital evolution*, springing from and corresponding with the evolution of faith.

Q. Where do they find any traces of this supposed vital evolution?

A. The traces of this evolution, they tell us, are

so visible in the books that one might almost write a history of them.

Q. Have the Modernists made an attempt to write this history of " vital evolution," which, according to their system, has controlled the successive additions to our Sacred Books?

A. Indeed, this history they do actually write, and with such an easy security that one might believe them to have with their own eyes seen the writers at work through the ages amplifying the Sacred Books.

Q. What means do the Modernists employ to confirm this history of the formation of the sacred text?

A. To aid them in this they call to their assistance that branch of criticism which they call *textual,* and labor to show that such a fact or such a phrase is not in its right place, and adducing other arguments of the same kind.

Q. What do you think of the assurance with which our Modernists proceed to explain the formation of our Sacred Books?

A. They seem, in fact, to have constructed for themselves certain types of narration and discourses, upon which they base their decision as to whether a thing is out of place or not.

Q. Are the Modernists not so bold and forward that we may ask them, " how are you fitted for practicing this kind of criticism?"

A. To hear them talk about their works on the

Sacred Books, in which they have been able to discover so much that is defective, one would imagine that before them nobody ever even glanced through the pages of Scripture, whereas the truth is that a whole multitude of Doctors, infinitely superior to them in genius, in erudition, in sanctity, have sifted the Sacred Books in every way.

Q. How did the ancient Doctors, who were infinitely superior to our Modernists, conduct themselves toward the Sacred Books?

A. So far from finding imperfections in them, they have thanked God more and more the deeper they have gone into them, for His divine bounty in having vouchsafed to speak thus to men.

Q. How do the Modernists ironically explain the respect which the ancient Doctors exhibited toward the Sacred Books?

A. Unfortunately, they say, these great Doctors did not enjoy the same aids to study that are possessed by the Modernists.

Q. What were these " aids to study" which the ancient Doctors had not, and which the Modernists enjoy?

A. These *aids* are simply philosophy borrowed from the negation of God, and a criterion which consists of themselves.

§5. *Conclusion.*

Q. What, in brief, is the historical method of the Modernist?

A. We believe, then, that We have set forth with sufficient clearness the historical method of the Modernists. The philosopher leads the way, the historian follows, and then in due order come internal and textual criticism.

Q. Since a certain philosophy forms the basis of the Modernist historical method, and is, as it were, its first cause, how may we rightly qualify their historical criticism?

A. Since it is characteristic of the first cause to communicate its virtue to secondary causes, it is quite clear that the criticism We are concerned with is an *agnostic, immanentist, and evolutionist* criticism.

Q. May this criticism be used without detriment to faith?

A. Anybody who embraces it and employs it, makes profession thereby of the errors contained in it, and places himself in opposition to Catholic faith.

Q. This being so, what shall be our judgment on the praise bestowed by certain Catholics on Modernist criticism?

A. One can not but be greatly surprised by the consideration which is attached to it by certain Catholics.

Q. Hence, why do certain Catholics allow themselves to give such value to a criticism which is contrary to their faith?

A. Two causes may be assigned for this: first, the

close alliance, independent of all differences of nationality or religion, which the historians and critics of this school have formed among themselves; second, the boundless effrontery of these men.

Q. Is there a bond of union among the Modernists of the several nations?

A. Yes. Let one of them but open his mouth and the others applaud him in chorus, proclaiming that science has made another step forward.

Q. Are they united against their critics?

A. Let an outsider but hint at a desire to inspect the new discovery with his own eyes, and they are on him in a body.

Q. What, in brief, are their tactics toward those who defend or attack any of their novelties?

A. Deny it—and you are an ignoramus; embrace it, defend it—and there is no praise too warm for you.

Q. Do these tactics attract the unwary?

A. In this way they win over many who, did they but realize what they are doing, would shrink back with horror.

Q. What has been the result of the domineering of the Modernists and the thoughtlessness of those who have been imposed upon?

A. The impudence and the domineering of some, and the thoughtlessness and imprudence of others, have combined to generate a pestilence in the air which penetrates everywhere and spreads the contagion. But let us pass to the apologist.

CHAPTER VI.

The Modernist as Apologist.

§1. *Principles and Sources.*

Q. Does the Modernist apologist also depend on the philosopher?

A. The Modernist apologist depends in two ways on the philosopher. First, *indirectly*, inasmuch as his theme is history—history dictated, as we have seen, by the philosopher; and, secondly, *directly*, inasmuch as he takes both his laws and his principles from the philosopher.

Q. What is the common precept of the Modernist school in the " new apologetics?"

A. Hence that common precept of the Modernist school that the new apologetics must be fed from psychological and historical sources.

Q. How do the Modernist apologists sacrifice to the rationalists the historical books which are " in current use in the Church?"

A. The Modernist apologists, then, enter the arena by proclaiming to the rationalists that though they are defending religion, they have no intention of employing the data of the Sacred Books or the histories in current use in the Church, and composed according to old methods, but *real* history written on modern principles and according to rigorously modern methods.

Q. Perhaps they speak thus by way of an "argumentum ad hominem" only, and not from personal convictions?

A. In all this they are *not* using an *argumentum ad hominem,* but are stating the simple fact that they hold, that the truth is to be found only in this kind of history.

Q. Do not the Modernists feel called upon to assure the rationalists of their sincerity?

A. They feel that it is not necessary for them to dwell on their own sincerity in their writings—they are already known to and praised by the rationalists as fighting under the same banner, and they not only plume themselves on these encomiums, which are a kind of salary to them, but would provoke nausea in a real Catholic.

Q. Do these rationalist encomiums arouse sentiments of disgust in the hearts of our Modernists?

A. No. They use them as an offset to the reprimands of the Church.

§2. *Application of Agnosticism.*

Q. In his apologetic, what does the Modernist set before himself?

A. The aim he sets before himself is to make the non-believer attain the *experience* of the Catholic religion.

Q. Why is the Modernist so anxious to produce this experience in the non-believer?

A. Because, according to the system, it is the basis of faith.

Q. How does the Modernist attain to a personal experience of the Catholic religion?

A. There are two ways open to him, the *objective* and the *subjective*.

Q. Whence proceeds the first or objective way?

A. The first of them proceeds from Agnosticism.

Q. What does this " first way " tend to show?

A. It tends to show that religion, and especially the Catholic religion, is endowed with such vitality as to *compel every psychologist* and historian of good faith to recognize that its history hides some unknown element.

Q. What must we first prove in order to show this?

A. To this end it is necessary to prove that this religion, as it exists to-day, is that which was founded by Jesus Christ; that is to say, that it is the product of the progressive development of the germ which He brought into the world.

Q. If Jesus Christ has brought into this world simply the germ of the Catholic religion, what is the first task of the Modernist?

A. It is imperative first of all to establish what this *germ* was.

Q. Give the Modernist formula for establishing what this germ was?

A. The Modernist claims to be able to do this by *the following formula:* Christ announced the coming of the kingdom of God, which was to be realized within in a brief lapse of time, and of which He was to become the Messias, the divinely-given agent and ordainer.

Q. The germ thus determined, what must be demonstrated, according to Modernist apologists?

A. Then it must be shown how this germ, always *immanent* and *permanent* in the bosom of the Church, has gone on slowly developing in the course of history, adapting itself successively to the different mediums through which it has passed, borrowing from them by *vital* assimilation all the dogmatic, cultual, ecclesiastical forms that served its purpose; whilst, on the other hand, it surmounted all obstacles, vanquished all enemies, and survived all assaults and all combats.

Q. Considering this mass of facts, at what conclusion do our Modernists hope to arrive?

A. Anybody who well and duly considers this mass of obstacles, adversaries, attacks, combats, and the vitality and fecundity which the Church has shown throughout them all, must admit that if the laws of evolution are visible in her life they fail to explain the whole of her history—the *unknown* rises forth from it and presents itself before us.

Q. What is the radical defect of all this reasoning?

A. Thus do they argue, never suspecting that their

determination of the primitive germ is an *a priori* of agnostic and evolutionist philosophy, and that the formula of it has been gratuitously invented for the sake of buttressing their position.

§3. *Application of Apologetic Principles.*

Q. Among the facts which they bring forth to secure access for the Catholic religion into souls, do not the Modernists find distasteful things?

A. While they endeavor, by this line of reasoning, to secure access for the Catholic religion into souls, these new apologists are quite ready to admit that there are many distasteful things in it.

Q. Surely they find the dogmas exempt from errors and contradictions?

A. Nay, they admit openly, and with ill-concealed satisfaction, that they have found that even its dogma is not exempt from errors and contradictions.

Q. You say they claim to have found errors and contradictions in dogma, and that they admit this with pleasure? At least they repudiate these errors and contradictions with indignation?

A. They add also that this is not only excusable but—curiously enough—even right and proper.

Q. Do our Modernists find errors in the Sacred Books?

A. In the Sacred Books there are many passages

referring to science or history where manifest errors are to be found.

Q. Admitting scientific and historical errors in the Bible, how do the Modernists apologize for the Sacred Books?

A. The subject of these books is not science or history, but religion and morals. In them history and science serve only as a species of covering, to enable the religious and moral experiences wrapped up in them to penetrate more readily among the masses. The masses understood science and history as they are expressed in these books, and it is clear that had science and history been expressed in a more perfect form, this would have proved rather a hindrance than a help.

Q. What other excuse do they offer to satisfy for the errors which they pretend to find in the Sacred Books?

A. The Sacred Books being essentially religious, are consequently necessarily living. Now life has its own truth and its own logic—quite different from rational truth and rational logic, belonging, as they do, to a different order, *viz.,* truth of adaptation and of proportion both with the medium in which it exists and with the end toward which it tends.

Q. Would not this show that the errors are true and legitimate, since they correspond to the necessity of vital adaptation?

A. The Modernists, losing all sense of control, go so far as to proclaim as true and legitimate everything that is explained by life.

Q. Can we thus legitimatize the "errors in our Sacred Books?"

A. We, for whom there is but one and only truth, and who hold that the Sacred Books, *written under the inspiration of the Holy Ghost, have God for their author* (Conc. Vat., *De Revel.*, c. 2) declare that this is equivalent to attributing to God Himself the lie of utility or officious lie, and we say with St. Augustine: *In an authority so high, admit but one officious lie, and there will not remain a single passage of those apparently difficult to practise or to believe, which on the same most pernicious rule may not be explained as a lie uttered by the author wilfully and to serve a purpose.* (Epist. 28.) And thus it will come about, the holy Doctor continues, that *everybody will believe and refuse to believe what he likes or dislikes.*

Q. Are the Modernists checked by the condemnations of the Church?

A. No. The Modernists pursue their way gaily.

Q. Give another example of the Modernists' shocking views in regard to our Sacred Books?

A. They grant also that certain arguments adduced in the Sacred Books, like those, for example, which are based on the prophecies, have no rational foundation to rest on.

Q. Do they attempt a still further justification of their errors?

A. They will defend even these as artifices of preaching, which are justified by life.

Q. Do they stop here?

A. No, indeed, for they are ready to admit, nay, to proclaim, that Christ Himself manifestly erred in determining the time when the coming of the kingdom of God was to take place.

Q. Do they dare say that Jesus Christ was deceived?

A. They tell us that we must not be surprised at this, since even Christ was subject to the laws of life!

Q. If Our Saviour Jesus Christ be convicted of error, what is to become of the dogmas of the Church?

A. The dogmas brim over with flagrant contradictions.

Q. How do our Modernists attempt to justify these flagrant contradictions in dogma?

A. What matters that, since, apart from the fact that vital logic accepts them, they are not repugnant to symbolical truth. Are we not dealing with the infinite, and has not the infinite an infinite variety of aspects?

Q. Do they not blush to thus justify contradictions?

A. Far from it! To maintain and defend these theories they do not hesitate to declare that the noblest homage that can be paid to the infinite is to make it the object of contradictory propositions!

Q. What do you think of such an excess?

A. When they justify even contradictions, what is it that they will refuse to justify?

§4. *Application of Immanence.*

Q. We have seen the objective means by which the Modernists hope to dispose the non-believer to faith. Have they no other way, no other argument?

A. It is not solely by *objective* arguments that the non-believer may be disposed to faith. There are also *subjective* ones at the disposal of the Modernists.

Q. Upon what philosophical doctrine do the Modernists base their subjective arguments?

A. For those they return to their doctrine of *immanence.* They endeavor, in fact, to persuade the non-believer that down in the very deeps of his nature and his life lie the need and the desire for religion.

Q. Is it simply for " a religion of any kind" that the Modernists find within us the " need and the desire?"

A. They find this *need and desire* within us not for a religion of any kind, but the specific religion known as Catholicism.

Q. By the doctrine of immanence how do the Modernists claim to find within us the " need and the desire" for a supernatural religion such as Catholicism?

A. They say this is absolutely *postulated* by the perfect development of life.

Q. What must we unite with His Holiness in deploring?

A. We can not but deplore once more, and grievously, that there are Catholics who, while rejecting *immanence* as a doctrine, employ it as a method of apologetics.

Q. Do not Catholic apologists extenuate the method of immanence, and do the Modernists not seek to find in human nature a something other than the mere capacity and suitability for the supernatural order?

A. They do, and this so imprudently that they seem to admit that there is in human nature a true and rigorous necessity with regard to the supernatural order—and not merely a capacity and a suitability for the supernatural, such as has at all times been emphasized by Catholic apologists.

Q. Are the Modernists, who hold this view, Modernists in the full sense of the word?

A. Truth to tell, it is only the moderate Modernists who make this appeal to an exigency for the Catholic religion.

Q. If these be "moderate," what shall we say of the other Modernists?

A. As for the others, who might be called *integralists,* they would show to the non-believer, hidden away in the very depths of his being, the very germ which Christ Himself bore in His conscience, and which He bequeathed to the world.

Q. From this summary description, what do you think of the Modernist apologetic method?

A. It is in perfect harmony, as you may see, with their doctrines.

Q. Why have such methods and doctrines been made?

A. These methods and doctrines, brimming over with errors, have been made *not for edification* but for destruction, not for the formation of Catholics, *but for the plunging of Catholics into heresy;* methods and doctrines that would be fatal to any religion.

CHAPTER VII.

The Modernist as Reformer.

Q. To complete the description of the Modernist character, what remains to be said?

A. It remains for Us now to say a few words about the Modernist as reformer.

Q. From what has preceded, can we not gain some idea of the "reforming mania" which possesses the Modernists?

A. From all that has preceded, some idea may be gained of the reforming mania which possesses them.

Q. Does this "reforming mania" extend to many things?

A. In all Catholicism there is absolutely nothing on which it does not fasten.

Q. Upon what first reform does the Modernists' attention "fasten?"

A. The reform of philosophy, especially in the seminaries.

Q. What is the character of the reform in philosophy which they hope to introduce into the seminaries?

A. Scholastic philosophy is to be relegated to the history of philosophy among obsolete systems, and the young men are to be taught modern philosophy.

Q. Why do they wish to teach modern philosophy in the seminaries?

A. Because it alone is true and suited to the times in which we live.

Q. Having reformed philosophy, for what further reform do the Modernists call?

A. The reform of theology.

Q. What reform do they demand for theology?

A. Rational theology is to have *modern philosophy* for its foundation, and positive theology is to be founded on the history of dogma.

Q. In history, what reform must be adopted?

A. As for history, it must be for the future written and taught only according to their modern methods and principles.

Q. Must dogma be subjected to a like reform?

A. Dogmas and their evolution are to be harmonized with science and history.

Q. What must be reformed in the Catechism?

A. In the *Catechism* no dogmas are to be inserted except those that have been duly reformed and are within the capacity of the people.

Q. In worship, what is to be reformed?

A. Regarding *worship,* the number of external devotions is to be reduced, or at least steps must be taken to prevent their further increase.

Q. Are not some Modernists more indulgent toward the ceremonies of worship?

A. Some of the admirers of symbolism are disposed to be more indulgent on this head.

Q. What reforms of a graver nature do the Modernists demand in the government of the Church?

A. Ecclesiastical government requires to be reformed in all its branches, but especially in its disciplinary and dogmatic parts. Its spirit and its external manifestations must be put in harmony with the public conscience, which is now wholly for democracy; a share in ecclesiastical government should therefore be given to the *lower ranks of the clergy,* and *even to the laity,* and authority should be *decentralized.*

Q. Do our Modernists require still further reforms?

A. Yes. The Roman Congregations, and especially the Index and the Holy Office, are to be reformed.

Q. What do they ask of the ecclesiastical authority in the " social and political world?"

A. The ecclesiastical authority must change its line of conduct in the social and political world; while keeping outside political and social organization, it must adapt itself to those which exist, in order to penetrate them with its spirit.

Q. What do the Modernists advocate in the moral world?

A. With regard to morals, they adopt the principle of the *Americanists,* that the active virtues are more important than the passive, both in the estimation in which they must be held and in the exercise of them.

Q. What are the clergy to do, according to Modernist principles?

A. The clergy are asked to return to their ancient lowliness and poverty, and in their ideas and action to be guided by the principles of Modernism.

Q. Advocating thus such virtues in the clergy, no doubt the Modernists exalt ecclesiastical celibacy?

A. There are some who, echoing the teaching of their Protestant masters, would like the suppression of ecclesiastical celibacy.

Q. Now that you have seen all the reforms demanded by the Modernists, what is left?

A. Indeed we may truly ask: *What is there left in the Church,* which is not to be reformed according to their principles?

CHAPTER VIII.

CRITICISM OF THE MODERNIST SYSTEM.

The Synthesis of all the Heresies. The Way to Atheism.

Q. Why have we exposed the Modernists' doctrines at such length?

A. It may be that some may think We have dwelt too long on this exposition of the doctrines of the Modernists.

Q. But why was this long exposition necessary?

A. It was necessary, both in order to refute their customary charge that We do not understand their ideas.

Q. Had we no other reason for thus exposing the system?

A. We had. We desired to show that their system does not consist in scattered and unconnected theories, *but in a perfectly organized body,* all the parts of which are solidly joined so that it is not possible to admit one without admitting all.

Q. Does this double motive explain the "didactic form," which we have used?

A. For this reason, too, We have had to give this exposition a *somewhat didactic form,* and not to shrink from employing certain uncouth terms in use among the Modernists.

CRITICISM OF THE MODERNIST SYSTEM

Q. Can Modernism, as a system, be defined in one word?

A. Can anybody, who takes a survey of the whole system, be surprised that We should define it as the *synthesis of all heresies?*

Q. Why do you define Modernism as the synthesis of all heresies?

A. Were one to attempt the task of collecting together all the errors that have been broached against the faith and to concentrate the sap and substance of them all into one, he could not better succeed than the Modernists have done.

Q. Is it enough to say that the Modernists, by their accumulated errors, destroy the Catholic religion?

A. Nay, they have done more than this, for, as We have already intimated, their system means the destruction not of the Catholic religion alone, but of all religion.

Q. Should not the rationalists applaud the Modernists?

A. With good reason the rationalists should applaud them, for the most sincere and the frankest among the rationalists warmly welcome the Modernists as their most valuable allies.

Q. Show how Modernists are the most efficient auxiliaries of the rationalists?

A. Let us return for a moment to that most disastrous doctrine of *Agnosticism.*

Q. Having closed, by Agnosticism, every avenue to God, how do the Modernists in their turn pretend to open the way to God?

A. By Agnosticism every avenue that leads the intellect to God is barred, but the Modernists would seek to open others available for sentiment and action.

Q. Do their efforts promise success?

A. No! Their efforts are vain.

Q. Why?

A. After all, what is sentiment but the reaction of the soul on the action of the intelligence or the senses?

Q. Since then, in order " to go to God," sentiment is directed either by the intellect or by the senses, what must happen if the Modernists take away the guidance of intelligence?

A. Take away the intelligence, and man, already inclined to follow the senses, becomes their slave.

Q. Is not this attempt " to go to God," through Agnostic sentiment, vain from another point of view?

A. Vain, too, it is from another point of view, for all these fantasies on the religious sentiment will never be able to destroy common sense, and common sense tells us that emotion and everything that leads the heart captive proves a hindrance instead of a help to the discovery of truth.

Q. What do you mean when you say that emotion and everything that leads the heart captive proves a hindrance to the discovery of the truth?

A. We speak, of course, of truth in itself.

Q. Can not the emotion of the soul aid in the discovery of even a vestige of truth?

A. Even for that other purely *subjective* truth, the fruit of sentiment and action, if it serves its purpose for the jugglery of words, *it is of no use* to the man who wants to know, above all things, whether outside himself there is a God into whose hands he is one day to fall.

Q. With Agnosticism as a point of departure, religious sentiment has no foot to stand on. To eke out their system, what do the Modernists add?

A. The Modernists call in *experience* to eke out their system, but what does this *experience* add to sentiment

Q. What does experience add to sentiment?

A. Absolutely nothing beyond a certain intensity and a proportionate deepening of the conviction of the reality of the object. But these two will never make sentiment into anything but sentiment, nor deprive it of its characteristic, which is to cause deception when the intelligence is not there to guide it; on the contrary, they but confirm and aggravate this characteristic, for the more intense sentiment is the more it is sentimental.

Q. In matters of religious sentiment and religious experience, are not prudence and knowledge extremely necessary?

A. In matters of religious sentiment and religious

experience, you know how necessary is prudence, and how necessary, too, the science which directs prudence. You know it from your own dealings with souls, and especially with souls in whom sentiment predominates; you know it also from your reading of ascetical books.

Q. Are ascetical works good guides in these matters, according to the Modernists?

A. No. Ascetical books, for which the Modernists have but little esteem, but testify to a science and a solidity very different from theirs, and to a refinement and subtlety of observation of which the Modernists give no evidence.

Q. Do you esteem, very highly, Modernist religious experience?

A. Is it not really folly, or at least sovereign imprudence, to trust one's self without control to Modernist experiences?

Q. Putting a question in passing, can an " argumentum ad hominem " be used against the Modernists, thus turning against them the proofs which they claim to derive from religious experience?

A. Let us for a moment put the question: If experiences have so much value in their eyes, why do they not attach equal weight to the experience that thousands upon thousands of Catholics have that the Modernists are on the wrong road? Is it, perchance, that all experiences except those felt by the Modernists are false and deceptive?

Q. Taking up once more the thread of the argument, what does the vast majority of mankind think of this sentiment and experience?

A. The vast majority of mankind holds and always will hold firmly that sentiment and experience alone, when not enlightened and guided by reason, *do not lead to the knowledge of God.*

Q. What remains?

A. What remains, then, but the annihilation of all religion—*atheism?*

Q. Since the doctrine of the Modernists on religious experience leads to atheism, do they not find in their " doctrine of symbolism " something to save them from this peril?

A. Certainly *it is not the doctrine of symbolism that will save us from this.* For if all the intellectual elements, as they call them, of religion are pure symbols, will not the very name of God or of divine personality be also a symbol, and if this be admitted will not the personality of God become a matter of doubt and the way opened to Pantheism?

Q. Is it only the Modernist doctrine of symbolism which leads to Pantheism?

A. To Pantheism that other doctrine of the *divine immanence* leads directly.

Q. Show us this consequence by an irrefutable argument?

A. For does it, We ask, leave God distinct from

man or not? If yes, in what does it differ from Catholic doctrine, and why reject external revelation? If no, we are at once in Pantheism. Now the doctrine of immanence in the Modernist acceptation holds and professes that every phenomenon of conscience proceeds from man as man. The rigorous conclusion from this is the identity of man with God, which means Pantheism.

Q. Does this Pantheistic conclusion follow from any other Modernist doctrine?

A. The same conclusion follows from the distinction Modernists make between science and faith.

Q. Be good enough to show this by formal argumentation?

A. The object of science, they say, is the reality of the knowable; the object of faith, on the contrary, is the reality of the unknowable. Now what makes the unknowable unknowable is its disproportion with the intelligible—a disproportion which nothing whatever, even in the doctrine of the Modernist, can suppress. Hence the unknowable remains and will eternally remain unknowable to the believer as well as to the man of science. Therefore, if any religion at all is possible it can only be the religion of an unknowable reality. And why this religion might not be that universal soul of the universe, of which a rationalist speaks, is something We do not see.

Q. Give your final conclusion?

A. Certainly this suffices to show superabundantly by how many roads Modernism leads to the annihilation of all religion.

Q. Describe the gradual descent of the human mind to the denial of all religion?

A. The *first* step in this direction was taken by *Protestantism;* the *second* is made by *Modernism;* the *next* will plunge headlong into *atheism.*

PART II

THE CAUSE OF MODERNISM

Q. To better understand Modernism, and to find suitable remedies, what must now be done?

A. To penetrate still deeper into Modernism, and to find a suitable remedy for such a deep sore, it behooves Us *to investigate the causes* which have engendered it and which foster its growth.

§1. *Moral Causes: Curiosity and Pride.*

Q. Give the proximate and immediate cause of Modernism?

A. That the proximate and immediate cause consists in a perversion of the mind can not be open to doubt.

Q. Perversion of mind is the proximate cause of Modernism; consequently where shall we find the remote cause?

A. The remote causes seem to Us to be reduced to two: curiosity and pride.

Q. Is curiosity really a cause of error?

A. Curiosity by itself, if not prudently regulated, *suffices to explain all errors.* Such is the opinion of Our Predecessor, Gregory XVI, who wrote: *A lamentable spectacle is that presented by the aberrations of human reason when it yields to the spirit of novelty, when against the warning of the Apostle, it seeks to know beyond what it is meant to know, and when, relying too much on itself, it thinks it can find the truth outside the Church wherein truth is found without the slightest shadow of error* (Ep. Encycl. *Singulari nos,* 7 Kal. Jul., 1834).

Q. What evil exercises greater sway than curiosity, blinds the soul, and plunges it into error?

A. It is pride which exercises an incomparably greater sway over the soul to blind it and plunge into error.

Q. Has pride invaded Modernist doctrines?

A. Pride sits in Modernism as in its own house, finding sustenance everywhere in its doctrines and an occasion to flaunt itself in all its aspects.

Q. Can you describe that pride which fills the Modernist?

A. It is pride which fills Modernists with that confidence in themselves and leads them to hold themselves up as the rule for all, pride which puffs them up with that vainglory which allows them to regard themselves as the sole possessors of knowledge, and makes them say, inflated with presumption, *We are not as the rest of men,* and which, to make them really not as other men, leads them to embrace all kinds of the most absurd novelties; it is pride which rouses in them the spirit of disobedience, and causes them to demand a compromise between authority and liberty; it is pride that makes of them the reformers of others, while they forget to reform themselves, and which begets their absolute want of respect for authority, not excepting the supreme authority.

Q. Is there any surer road to Modernism than pride?

A. No, truly, there is no road which leads so directly to Modernism as pride.

Q. Shall the Catholic, priest or layman, who is puffed up by pride, infallibly become a Modernist?

A. When a Catholic layman or a priest forgets that precept of the Christian life which obliges us to renounce ourselves if we would follow Jesus Christ and neglects to tear pride from his heart, ah! but he is a *fully ripe subject* for the errors of Modernism.

Q. What is the duty of the Bishops in regard to proud priests?

A. Your first duty, says the Holy Father to the Bishops, will be to thwart such proud men, to employ them only in the lowest and obscurest offices; the higher they try to rise, the lower let them be placed, so that their lowly position may deprive them of the power of causing damage.

Q. Are not directors of seminaries under an equal obligation to reject from the priesthood any young cleric who is tainted with pride?

A. Sound your young clerics, too, most carefully, by yourselves and by the directors of your seminaries, and when you find the spirit of pride among any of them *reject them without compunction* from the priesthood.

Q. Has this duty of exercising proper vigilance in rejecting proud men from the priesthood always been observed in the past?

A. Would to God that this had always been done with the proper vigilance and constancy.

§2. *Intellectual Causes.*

Q. Passing from these two moral causes, curiosity and pride, what is the chief intellectual cause of Modernism?

A. If we pass from the moral to the intellectual causes of Modernism, the first which presents itself, and the chief one, is ignorance.

Q. Surely you do not stigmatize Modernists, those men who pose as Doctors of the Church, as ignorant men?

A. Yes, these very Modernists who pose as Doctors of the Church, who puff out their cheeks when they speak of modern philosophy, and show such contempt for scholasticism, have embraced the one with all its false glamor because their ignorance of the other has left them without the means of being able to recognize confusion of thought, and to refute sophistry.

Q. Has not this false Modernist philosophy, be-

cause of its ignorance of scholastic philosophy, given birth to Modernism itself?

A. The whole system, with all its errors, has been born of the alliance between faith and false philosophy.

§3. *Artifices Employed by the Modernists to Disseminate their Errors.*

Q. Are not the Modernists "zealous in propagating" their pernicious system?

A. If only they had displayed less zeal and energy in propagating it! But such is their activity and such their unwearying capacity for work on behalf of their cause, that one can not but be pained to see them waste such labor in endeavoring to ruin the Church when they might have been of such service to her had their efforts been better employed.

Q. In this active propaganda for the spread of their system, do the Modernists make use of artifices?

A. Their artifices to delude men's minds are of two kinds.

Q. What are the two kinds of artifices employed by the Modernists?

A. Their first is to remove obstacles from their path, the second is to devise and apply actively and patiently every instrument that can serve their purpose.

(a) Negative Means.

Q. Do the Modernists admit that any obstacles are to be removed?

A. Yes. They admit three chief difficulties which bar the way.

Q. What are the three chief difficulties which the Modernist is forced to overcome?

A. The Modernists recognize that the three chief difficulties for them are scholastic philosophy, the authority of the Fathers and Tradition, and the magisterium of the Church.

Q. Do the Modernists really make war upon these?

A. On these they wage unrelenting war.

Q. What is the Modernists' appreciation of scholastic philosophy?

A. For scholastic philosophy and theology they have only ridicule and contempt.

Q. Do ridicule and contempt for scholastic philosophy go hand in hand with Modernism?

A. Whether it is *ignorance or fear*, or both, that inspires this conduct in them, certain it is that the passion for novelty is always united in them with hatred of scholasticism, and there is no surer sign that a man is on the way to Modernism than when he begins to show his dislike for this system.

Q. When the Modernists exhibit contempt for scholastic philosophy, of what should we remind them?

A. Modernists and their admirers should remember the proposition condemned by Pius IX: *The method and principles which have served the Doctors of scholasticism when treating of theology no longer correspond*

*with the exigencies of our time or the progress of
science* (Syll. Prop., 13).

*Q. In their war against scholastic philosophy, how
do the Modernists deal with the second obstacle, as
they call Tradition?*

A. They exercise all their ingenuity in diminishing
the force and falsifying the character of Tradition,
so as to rob it of all its weight.

*Q. In speaking of Tradition, what law of the sec-
ond Council of Nicea should true Catholics have in
mind?*

A. But for Catholics the second Council of Nicea
will always have the force of law, where it condemns
those *who dare, after the impious fashion of heretics,
to deride the ecclesiastical traditions, to invent novelties of some kind . . . or endeavor by malice or
craft to overthrow any one of the legitimate traditions
of the Catholic Church.*

*Q. Give the law of the fourth Council of Constan-
tinople on Tradition?*

A. Catholics will hold for law, also, the profession
of the fourth Council of Constantinople: *We, therefore, profess to conserve and guard the rules bequeathed to the Holy Catholic and Apostolic Church
by the Holy and most illustrious Apostles, by the orthodox Councils, both general and local, and by every
one of those divine interpreters, the Fathers and Doctors of the Church.*

Q. Does not the "profession of faith" include respect for Tradition?

A. Wherefore the Roman Pontiffs, Pius IV and Pius IX, ordered the insertion in the profession of faith of the following declaration: *I most firmly admit and embrace the apostolic and ecclesiastical traditions and other observances and constitutions of the Church.*

Q. Since they show such slight respect for Tradition, what is the judgment of the Modernists on the "most holy Fathers of the Church?"

A. The Modernists pass the same judgment on the most holy Fathers of the Church as they pass on Tradition, decreeing, with amazing effrontery, that, while personally most worthy of all veneration, they were entirely *ignorant* of history and criticism, for which they are only excusable on account of the time in which they lived.

Q. In what presumptuous way do the Modernists speak of the Fathers of the Church?

A. Finally, the Modernists try in every way to diminish and weaken the authority.

Q. In the war against scholastic philosophy and Tradition, what is the third obstacle which the Modernists feel obliged to remove?

A. They propose to remove the ecclesiastical magisterium itself by sacrilegiously falsifying its origin, character, and rights, and by freely repeating the calumnies of its adversaries.

Q. In their war against the "magisterium of the Church," may we not apply to the Modernists the earlier condemnations?

A. To all the band of Modernists may be applied those words which Our Predecessor wrote with such pain: *To bring contempt and odium on the mystic Spouse of Christ, who is the true light, the children of darkness have been wont to cast in her face before the world a stupid calumny, and perverting the meaning and force of things and words, to depict her as the friend of darkness and ignorance, and the enemy of light, science, and progress* (Motu proprio *Ut mysticum,* 14 March, 1891).

Q. Since the Modernists display such hatred against the Church, what is their attitude toward Catholics who defend her?

A. The Modernists vent all their gall and hatred on Catholics who sturdily fight the battles of the Church.

Q. What is the favorite insult offered by the Modernists to faithful Catholics?

A. Of all the insults they heap on them those of ignorance and obstinacy are the favorites.

Q. If the Catholic who defends the Church is a learned man, what tactics do the Modernists employ against him?

A. When an adversary rises up against them with an erudition and force that render him redoubtable,

they try to make a conspiracy of silence around him
to nullify the effects of his attack.

*Q. Contrast the conduct of the Modernists toward
the Catholic champion with the methods displayed
toward their own partisans?*

A. While in flagrant contrast with this policy
toward Catholics, they load with constant praise the
writers who range themselves on their side, hailing
their works, exuding novelty in every page, with
choruses of applause.

*Q. How do the Modernists gage the learning of
an author?*

A. For them the scholarship of a writer is in direct
proportion to the recklessness of his attacks on antiquity, and of his efforts to undermine Tradition and
the ecclesiastical magisterium.

*Q. When a Modernist falls under the condemna-
tions of the Church, are his fellows bold enough to sup-
port him?*

A. When one of their number falls under the condemnations of the Church the rest of them, to the
horror of good Catholics, gather round him, heap
public praise upon him, venerate him almost as a
martyr to truth.

*Q. Are the young excited and confused by this
Modernist uproar?*

A. The young, excited and confused by all this
clamor of praise and abuse, some of them afraid of

being branded as ignorant, others ambitious to be considered learned, and both classes goaded internally by curiosity and pride, often surrender, and give themselves up to Modernism.

Q. Is not this Modernist method of seducing the young, by noise and clamor, one of the artifices of conquest described above?

A. Yes. We have already seen some of the artifices employed by Modernists to exploit their wares.

(b) Positive Means.

Q. Are the Modernists active in seeking new recruits?

A. What efforts they make to win new recruits!

Q. What are the Modernists' chief means of conquest?

A. They seize upon chairs in the seminaries and universities, and gradually make of them chairs of pestilence. From these sacred chairs they scatter, though not always openly, the seeds of their doctrines; they proclaim their teachings without disguise in congresses; they introduce them and make them the vogue in social institutions. Under their own names and under pseudonyms they publish numbers of books, newspapers, reviews, and sometimes one and the same writer adopts a variety of pseudonyms to trap the incautious reader into believing in a whole multitude of Modernist writers—in short, they leave nothing untried, in action, discourses, writings, as though there were a frenzy of propaganda upon them.

Q. And the results of all this?

A. We have to lament at the sight of many young men, once full of promise and capable of rendering great services to the Church, now gone astray.

Q. What are the results of this activity?

A. And there is another sight that saddens Us too: that of so many other Catholics, who, while they certainly do not go so far as the former, have yet grown into the habit, as though they had been *breathing a poisoned atmosphere,* of thinking and speaking and writing with a liberty that ill becomes Catholics.

Q. Are Modernists found only among the laity?

A. They are to be found among the laity, and in the ranks of the clergy, and they are not wanting even in the last place where one might expect to meet them, in religious institutes.

Q. How do these more or less Modernist Catholics, either laymen, priests, or religious, treat biblical questions?

A. If they treat of biblical questions, it is upon Modernist principles.

Q. How do they deal with history?

A. If they write history, it is to search out with curiosity and to publish openly, on the pretext of telling the whole truth and with a species of ill-concealed satisfaction, everything that looks to them like a stain in the history of the Church.

Q. How do they act toward pious popular traditions and venerable relics?

A. Under the sway of certain *a priori* rules, they destroy, as far as they can, the pious traditions of the people, and bring ridicule on certain relics highly venerable from their antiquity.

Q. Why do they wish to break away from the ancient traditions?

A. They are possessed by the empty desire of being talked about, and they know they would never succeed in this were they to say only what has been always said.

Q. Are not these moderate Modernist Catholics actuated by good intentions in breaking away from the traditions of past ages?

A. It may be that they have persuaded themselves that in all this they are really serving God and the Church.

Q. In reality, what are they doing?

A. In reality they only offend both, less perhaps by their works themselves than by the spirit in which they write, and by the encouragement they are giving to the extravagances of the Modernists.

PART III

REMEDIES

Q. What action did Leo XIII take against the errors of the Modernists?

A. Against this host of grave errors, and its secret and open advance, Our Predecessor, Leo XIII, of happy memory, worked strenuously, especially as regards the Bible, both in his words and his acts.

Q. Were the Modernists deterred by his words and acts?

A. As we have seen, the Modernists are not easily deterred by such weapons—with an affectation of submission and respect, *they proceeded to twist the words of the Pontiff* to their own sense, and his acts they described as directed against others than themselves. And the evil has gone on increasing from day to day.

Q. What determination did the Holy Father, Pius X, reach?

A. He says: We, therefore, have determined to adopt at once the most efficacious measures in Our power.

Q. In what terms did he appeal to the Bishops, pastors of souls, educators, and chief superiors of religious institutes?

A. Pius X thus spoke to the Bishops, pastors, educators, and religious superiors: We beg and conjure you to see to it that in this most grave matter nobody will ever be able to say that you have been in the slightest degree wanting in vigilance, zeal, or firmness. And what We ask of you and expect of you, We ask and expect also of all other pastors of souls, of all educators and professors of clerics, and in a very special way of the superiors of religious institutions.

§1. *Rules for Study.*

Q. What does the Holy Father will and ordain on the subject of philosophy?

A. He says: In the first place, with regard to studies, We will and ordain that scholastic philosophy be made the basis of the sacred sciences.

Q. Following Leo XIII, how does Pius X limit his prescriptions?

A. Again he says: It goes without saying that *if anything is met with among the scholastic Doctors, which may be regarded as an excess of subtlety, or which is altogether destitute of probability, We have no desire whatever to propose it for the imitation of present generations* (Leo XIII, Enc. *Aeterni Patris*).

Q. What is the scholastic philosophy prescribed for seminaries and religious institutions?

A. Let it be clearly understood above all things that the scholastic philosophy We prescribe is that which the Angelic Doctor has bequeathed to us, and We, therefore, declare that all the ordinances of Our

Predecessor on this subject continue fully in force, and, as far as may be necessary, We do decree anew, and confirm, and ordain that they be by all strictly observed. In seminaries where they may have been neglected let the Bishops impose them and require their observance, and let this apply also to the superiors of religious institutions.

Q. Does there exist a prejudice against St. Thomas? May he be lightly set aside?

A. Let professors remember that they can not set St. Thomas aside, especially in metaphysical questions, without grave detriment.

Q. In what words does Pius X recommend the study of theology?

A. On this philosophical foundation the theological edifice is to be solidly raised. Promote the study of theology by all means in your power, so that your clerics on leaving the seminaries may admire and love it, and always find their delight in it. *For in the vast and varied abundance of studies opening before the mind desirous of truth, everybody knows how the old maxim describes theology as so far in front of all others that every science and art should serve it and be to it as handmaidens* (Leo XIII, Litt. ap. *In Magna,* Dec. 10, 1889).

Q. Does not the Holy Father praise those theologians who teach positive theology?

A. We will add that We deem worthy of praise

those who, with full respect for Tradition, the Holy Fathers, and the ecclesiastical magisterium, undertake, with well-balanced judgment and guided by Catholic principles (which is not always the case), to seek to illustrate positive theology by throwing the light of true history upon it.

Q. What method must be employed by those who treat positive theology?

A. Certainly *more attention must be paid to positive theology than in the past*, but this must be done without detriment to scholastic theology, and those are to be disapproved as of Modernist tendencies who exalt positive theology in such a way as to seem to despise the scholastic.

Q. By what law must the study of the natural sciences be regulated?

A. With regard to profane studies suffice it to recall here what Our Predecessor has admirably said: *Apply yourselves energetically to the study of natural sciences: the brilliant discoveries and the bold and useful applications of them made in our times which have won such applause by our contemporaries will be an object of perpetual praise for those that come after us* (Leo XIII, Alloc., March 7, 1880). But this do without interfering with sacred studies, as Our Predecessor in these most grave words prescribed: *If you carefully search for the cause of errors you will find that it lies in the fact that in these days when the natural sciences absorb so much study, the more severe and lofty studies have been proportionately neglected— some of them have almost passed into oblivion, some of them are pursued in a half-hearted or superficial way, and, sad to say, now that they are fallen from their old estate, they have been disfigured by perverse doctrines and monstrous errors* (*Loc. cit.*). We ordain, therefore, that the study of natural science in the seminaries be carried on under this law.

§2. *The Choice of Directors and Professors for Seminaries and Catholic Universities.*

Q. What prudence is to be exercised, and what rules are to be followed in the choice of professors for seminaries and Catholic universities?

A. All these prescriptions and those of Our Predecessors are to be borne in mind whenever there is question of choosing directors and professors for seminaries and Catholic universities. *Anybody who in any way is found to be imbued with Modernism is to be excluded without compunction* from these offices, and those who already occupy them are to be withdrawn. The same policy is to be adopted toward those who favor Modernism either by extolling the Modernists or excusing their culpable conduct, by criticizing scholasticism, the Holy Fathers, or by refusing obedience to ecclesiastical authority in any of its depositaries; and toward those who show a love of novelty in history, archæology, biblical exegesis, and finally toward those who neglect the sacred sciences or appear to prefer to them the profane. In all this question of studies, you can not be too watchful or too constant, but most of all in the choice of professors, for as a rule the students are modelled after the pattern of their masters. Strong in the consciousness of your duty, act always prudently but vigorously.

§3. *Rules for Students.*

Q. What diligence should be shown in selecting candidates for Holy Orders?

A. Equal diligence and severity are to be used in examining and selecting candidates for Holy Orders. Far, far from the clergy be the love of novelty! GOD HATES THE PROUD AND THE OBSTINATE.

Q. In order to be valid, upon what new condition shall the doctorate in theology and in philosophy be conferred?

A. For the future the doctorate of theology and canon law must never be conferred on anybody who has not made the regular course of scholastic philosophy; if conferred it shall be held as null and void.

Q. What rules laid down for the clergy of Italy, both regular and secular, are henceforth extended to all nations?

A. The rules laid down in 1896 by the Sacred Congregation of Bishops and Regulars for the clerics, both secular and regular, of Italy, concerning the frequenting of the universities, We now decree to be extended to all nations.

Q. What further command does the Sovereign Pontiff enjoin?

A. Clerics and priests inscribed in a Catholic institute or university *must not in the future follow in civil universities those courses for which there are chairs in the Catholic institutes to which they belong.* If this has been permitted anywhere in the past, We ordain that it be not allowed for the future.

Q. What is the obligation of the Bishops who form the governing board of Catholic universities and institutes?

A. Let the Bishops who form the governing board of such Catholic institutes or universities watch with all care that these Our commands be constantly observed.

§4. *On the Reading of Bad Books.*

Q. What is the duty of the Bishops in regard to writings infected with Modernism?

A. It is the duty of the Bishops to prevent writings infected with Modernism or favorable to it from being read when they have been published, and to hinder their publication when they have not.

Q. How must the Bishops proceed in the seminaries and universities?

A. No book or paper or periodical of this kind must ever be permitted to seminarists or university students. The injury to them would be equal to that caused by immoral reading—nay, it would be greater, for such writings poison Christian life at its very fount.

Q. Should the same action be taken concerning the writings of Catholics who are imbued with modern philosophy, and who are ill-instructed in theological studies?

A. The same decision is to be taken concerning the writings of some Catholics, who, though not badly disposed themselves, but ill-instructed in theological studies and imbued with modern philosophy, strive to make this harmonize with the faith, and, as they say, to turn it to the account of the faith. The name and reputation of these authors cause them to be read without suspicion, and they are, therefore, all the more dangerous in preparing the way for Modernism.

Q. Are the Bishops obliged to publicly and solemnly condemn pernicious books which have been circulated in their dioceses?

A. To give you some more general directions, in a matter of such moment, We bid you do everything in your power to drive out of your diocese, *even by solemn interdict,* any pernicious books that may be in circulation there. The Holy See neglects no means to put down writings of this kind, but the number of them has now grown to such an extent that it is impossible to censure them all. Hence it happens that the medicine sometimes arrives too late, for the disease has taken root during the delay. We will, therefore, that the Bishops, putting aside all fear and the prudence of the flesh, despising the outcries of the wicked, gently by all means, but constantly, do each his own share of this work, remembering the injunctions of Leo XIII in the Apostolic Constitution *Officiorum:* *Let the Ordinaries, acting in this also as Delegates of the Apostolic See, exert themselves to prescribe and to put out of reach of the faithful injurious books or other writings printed or circulated in their dioceses.* In this passage the Bishops, it is true, receive a right, but they have also a duty imposed on them. Let no Bishop think that he fulfils this duty by denouncing to us one or two books, while a great many others of the same kind are being published and circulated.

Q. Is it allowable, nay, rather, is it not at times the duty of the Bishops to condemn books which have obtained the Imprimatur?

A. You are not to be deterred, says Pius X to the Bishops, by the fact that a book has obtained the *Imprimatur* elsewhere, both because this may be merely simulated, and because it may have been granted through carelessness or easiness or excessive confidence in the author, as may sometimes happen in religious orders. Besides, just as the same food does

not agree equally with everybody, it may happen that
a book harmless in one, may, on account of the different
circumstances, be hurtful in another. Should a Bishop,
therefore, after having taken the advice of prudent
persons, deem it right to condemn any of such books
in his diocese, We not only give him ample faculty to
do so, but We impose it upon him as a duty to do so.
Of course, it is Our wish that in such action proper
regard be used, and sometimes it will suffice to restrict
the prohibition to the clergy.

*Q. When the restriction is directed to the clergy
only, may Catholic booksellers continue to put on sale
the condemned books?*

A. Even in such cases it will be obligatory on Catholic booksellers not to put on sale books condemned
by the Bishop.

*Q. Give the obligations of Bishops in regard to
Catholic booksellers?*

A. While we are on this subject of booksellers,
We wish the Bishops to see to it that they do not,
through desire for gain, put on sale unsound books.
It is certain that in the catalogues of some of them the
books of the Modernists are not unfrequently announced with no small praise. *If they refuse obedience, let the Bishops have no hesitation in depriving
them of the title of Catholic booksellers;* so, too, and
with more reason, if they have the title of Episcopal
booksellers, and if they have that of Pontifical, let them

be denounced to the Apostolic See. Finally, We remind all of the XXVI article of the above-mentioned Constitution *Officiorum*: *All those who have obtained an apostolic faculty to read and keep forbidden books, are not thereby authorized to read books and periodicals forbidden by the local Ordinaries, unless the apostolic faculty expressly concedes permission to read and keep books condemned by anybody.*

§5. *Diocesan Censors.*

Q. How should the Bishops deal with publications?

A. It is not enough to hinder the reading and the sale of bad books—it is also necessary to prevent them from being printed. Hence let the Bishops use the utmost severity in granting permission to print.

Q. Must official censors be appointed?

A. Under the rules of the Constitution *Officiorum*, many publications require the authorization of the Ordinary, and in some dioceses it has been made the custom to have a suitable number of official censors for the examination of writings. We have the highest praise for this institution, and We not only exhort, but We order that it be extended to all dioceses. In all episcopal Curias, therefore, let Censors be appointed for the revision of works intended for publication, and let the Censors be chosen from both ranks of the clergy —secular and regular—men of age, knowledge and prudence, who will know how to follow the golden mean in their judgments.

Q. What is the office of the official Censors?

A. It shall be their office to examine everything which requires permission for publication according to Articles XLI and XLII of the above-mentioned Constitution. The Censor shall give his verdict in writing. If it be favorable, the Bishop will give the permission for publication by the word *Imprimatur,* which must always be preceded by the *Nihil obstat* and the name of the Censor.

Q. Are official Censors to be appointed also for the Curia of Rome?

A. In the Curia of Rome official censors shall be appointed just as elsewhere, and the appointment of them shall appertain to the Master of the Sacred Palaces, after they have been proposed to the Cardinal Vicar and accepted by the Sovereign Pontiff. It will also be the office of the Master of the Sacred Palaces to select the Censor for each writing. Permission for publication will be granted by him as well as by the Cardinal Vicar or his Vicegerent, and this permission, as above prescribed, must always be preceded by the *Nihil obstat* and the name of the Censor.

Q. Is it ever allowable to omit the name of the Censor?

A. Only on very rare and exceptional occasions, and the prudent decision of the Bishop, shall it be possible to omit mention of the Censor.

Q. What precautions should be taken to protect the Censor?

A. The name of the Censor *shall never be made known to the authors until he shall have given a favorable decision,* so that he may not have to suffer annoyance either while he is engaged in the examination of a writing, or in case he should deny his approval.

Q. Under what conditions may Censors be chosen from the religious orders?

A. Censors shall never be chosen from the religious orders until the opinion of the Provincial, or in Rome of the General, has been privately obtained, and the Provincial or the General must give a conscientious account of the character, knowledge, and orthodoxy of the candidate.

Q. What approbations should books published by religious carry?

A. We admonish religious superiors of their solemn duty never to allow anything to be published by any of their subjects without permission from themselves and from the Ordinary.

Q. Is it permissible for the Censor to rely on his title for the defence of his personal opinions?

A. We affirm and declare that the title of Censor has no value and can never be adduced to give credit to the private opinions of the persons who hold it.

§6. Priests as Editors or Correspondents.

Q. May the members of the clergy, secular or regular, undertake the direction of papers or periodicals without the consent of the Ordinary?

A. Having said this much in general, We now ordain in particular a more careful observance of Article XLII of the above-mentioned Constitution *Officiorum.* It is *forbidden to secular priests, without the previous consent of the Ordinary, to undertake the direction of papers or periodicals.* This permission shall be withdrawn from any priest who makes a wrong use of it after having been admonished.

Q. With regard to priests who are correspondents or collaborators of periodicals, how are Bishops to act?

A. With regard to priests who are *correspondents* or *collaborators* of periodicals, as it happens not unfrequently that they write matter infected with Modernism for their papers or periodicals, let the Bishops see to it that this is not permitted to happen, and, should it happen, let them warn the writers or prevent them from writing.

Q. Should the superiors of religious orders fail in this duty, how are the Bishops to proceed?

A. The superiors of religious orders, too, We admonish with all authority to do the same, and should they fail in this duty let the Bishops make due provision with authority delegated by the Supreme Pontiff.

Q. Should a special Censor be appointed for each newspaper and periodical? What is his office? What is the Bishop's right?

A. Let there be, as far as this is possible, a special

Censor for newspapers and periodicals written by Catholics. It shall be his office to read in due time each number after it has been published, and if he finds anything dangerous in it let him order that it be corrected. The Bishop shall have the same right, even when the Censor has seen nothing objectionable in a publication.

§7. *Sacerdotal Congresses.*

Q. What rules are to be imposed on priests who wish to organize or participate in sacerdotal congresses?

A. We have already mentioned congresses and public gatherings as among the means used by the Modernists to propagate and defend their opinions. In the future, Bishops shall not permit congresses of priests except on very rare occasions. When they do permit them it shall only be on condition that matters appertaining to the Bishops or the Apostolic See be not treated in them, and that no motions or postulates be allowed that would imply a usurpation of sacred authority, and that no mention be made in them of Modernism, presbyterianism, or laicism. At congresses of this kind, which can only be held after permission in writing has been obtained in due time and for each case, it shall not be lawful for priests of other dioceses to take part without the written permission of their Ordinary. Further, no priest must lose sight of the solemn recommendation of Leo XIII: *Let priests hold as sacred the authority of their pastors, let them take it for certain that the sacerdotal ministry, if not exercised under the guidance of the Bishops, can never be either holy, or very fruitful or respectable.* (Litt. Encyc. *Nobilissima Gallorum*, 10 Feb., 1884.)

§8. *Diocesan Councils of Vigilance.*

Q. Give the words in which His Holiness, Pius X, commands the formation of " Councils of Vigilance" in every diocese?

A. Of what avail will be all Our commands and prescriptions if they be not dutifully and firmly carried out? And, in order that this may be done, it has seemed expedient to Us to extend to all dioceses the regulations laid down with great wisdom many years ago by the Bishops of Umbria for theirs.

" In order," they say, " to extirpate the errors already propagated and to prevent their further diffusion, and to remove those teachers of impiety through whom the pernicious effects of such diffusion are being perpetuated, this sacred Assembly, following the example of St. Charles Borromeo, has decided to establish in each of the dioceses a Council consisting of approved members of both branches of the clergy, which shall be charged with the task of noting the existence of errors and the devices by which new ones are introduced and propagated, and to inform the Bishop of the whole so that he may take counsel with them as to the best means for nipping the evil in the bud and preventing it spreading for the ruin of souls, or, worse still, gaining strength and growth " (Acts of the Congress of the Bishops of Umbria, Nov., 1849, tit. 2, art. 6). We decree, therefore, that in every diocese a Council of this kind, which We are pleased to name the " Council of Vigilance," be instituted without delay.

Q. How are the members of the " Council of Vigilance" to be chosen?

A. The priests called to form part in it shall be chosen somewhat after the manner above prescribed for the Censors.

Q. When shall they meet? Shall they be bound to secrecy?

A. They shall meet every two months on an appointed day under the presidency of the Bishop. They shall be bound to secrecy as to their deliberations and decisions.

Q. What are their duties?

A. Their function shall be as follows: *They shall watch most carefully for every trace and sign of Modernism* both in publications and in teaching, and, to preserve from it the clergy and the young, they shall take all prudent, prompt and efficacious measures.

Q. What should be the particular object of their attention?

A. Let them combat novelties of words, remembering the admonitions of Leo XIII (Instruct. S. C. NN. EE. EE., 27 Jan., 1902): *It is impossible to approve in Catholics of a style inspired by unsound novelty which seems to deride the piety of the faithful and dwells on the introduction of a new order of Christian life, on new directions of the Church, on new aspirations of the modern soul, on a new vocation of the clergy, on a new Christian civilization.* Language of this kind is not to be tolerated either in books or from chairs of learning.

Q. Should they observe books which treat of pious local traditions and of sacred relics?

A. The Councils must not neglect the books treating of the pious traditions of different places or of sacred relics. Let them not permit such questions to be discussed in periodicals destined to stimulate piety, neither with expressions savoring of mockery or contempt, nor by dogmatic pronouncements, especially when, as is often the case, what is stated as a certainty either does not pass the limits of probability or is merely based on prejudiced opinion.

Q. What rules are to be followed concerning sacred relics?

A. Concerning sacred relics, let this be the rule: When Bishops, who alone are judges in such matters, know for certain that a relic is not genuine, let them remove it at once from the veneration of the faithful;

if the authentications of a relic happen to have been lost through civil disturbances, or in any other way, let it not be exposed for public veneration until the Bishop has verified it. The argument of prescription or well-founded presumption is to have weight only when devotion to a relic is commendable by reason of its antiquity, according to the sense of the Decree issued in 1896 by the Congregation of Indulgences and Sacred Relics: *Ancient relics are to retain the veneration they have always enjoyed except when in individual instances there are clear arguments that they are false or supposititious.*

Q. In passing judgment on pious traditions, what must be borne in mind?

A. In passing judgment on pious traditions be it always borne in mind that in this matter the Church uses the greatest prudence, and that she does not allow traditions of this kind to be narrated in books except with the utmost caution and with the insertion of the declaration imposed by Urban VIII, and even then she does not guarantee the truth of the fact narrated; she simply does not forbid belief in things for which human arguments are not wanting. On this matter the Sacred Congregation of Rites, thirty years ago, decreed as follows: *These apparitions and revelations have neither been approved nor condemned by the Holy See, which has simply allowed that they be believed on purely human faith, on the tradition which they relate, corroborated by testimonies and documents worthy of credence* (Decree, May 2, 1877). Anybody who follows this rule has no cause for fear. For the devotion based on any apparition, in as far as it regards the fact itself, that is to say in as far as it is *relative,* always implies the hypothesis of the truth of the fact; while in as far as it is absolute, it must always be based on the truth, seeing that its object is the persons of the saints who are honored. The same is true of relics.

Q. Is it, in fine, the duty of the " Council of Vigilance" to supervise social institutions and writings on social questions?

A. Finally, We entrust to the Councils of Vigilance the duty of overlooking assiduously and diligently social institutions as well as writings on social questions so that they may harbor no trace of Modernism, but obey the prescriptions of the Roman Pontiffs.

§9. *Triennial Returns.*

Q. What injunction has the Sovereign Pontiff laid upon all Bishops and superiors-general of religious orders?

A. Lest what We have laid down thus far should fall into oblivion, We will and ordain that the Bishops of all dioceses, a year after the publication of these letters and every three years thenceforward, furnish the Holy See with a diligent and sworn report on all the prescriptions contained in them, and on the doctrines that find currency among the clergy, and especially in the seminaries and other Catholic institutions, and We impose the like obligation on the generals of religious orders with regard to those under them.

CONCLUSION

The Church and Scientific Progress.

This is what We have thought it Our duty to write to you for the salvation of all who believe. The adversaries of the Church will doubtless abuse what We have said to refurbish the old calumny by which We are traduced as the enemy of science and of the progress of humanity. In order to oppose a new answer to such accusations, which the history of the Christian religion refutes by never-failing arguments, it is Our intention to establish and develop by every means in Our power a special institute in which, through the cooperation of those Catholics who are most eminent for their learning, the progress of science and other realms of knowledge may be promoted under the guidance and teaching of Catholic truth. God grant that We may happily realize Our design with the ready assistance of all those who bear a sincere love for the Church of Christ. But of this We will speak on another occasion.

Meanwhile, fully confident in your zeal and work, We beseech for you with Our whole heart and soul the abundance of heavenly light, so that in the midst of this great perturbation of men's minds from the insidious invasions of error from every side, you may see clearly what you ought to do and may perform the task with all your strength and courage. May Jesus Christ, the author and finisher of our faith, be with you by His power; and may the Immaculate Virgin, the destroyer of all heresies, be with you by her prayers and aid. And We, as a pledge of Our affection and of divine assistance in adversity, grant most affectionately and with all Our heart to you, your clergy and people, the Apostolic Benediction.

Given at St. Peter's, Rome, on the 8th day of September, 1907, the fifth year of Our Pontificate.

PIUS X, POPE.

Order from your bookdealer or directly from the publisher.

NOTES

NOTES